WILEY CIAexcel EXAM REVIEW

FOCUS
NOTES
2018

WILEY CIAexcel EXAM REVIEW

FOCUS NOTES 2018

PART 2
Internal Audit Practice

S. RAO VALLABHANENI

WILEY

Library of Congress Cataloging-in-Publication Data:

ISBN 978-1-119-48295-6 (Paperback); ISBN 978-1-119-48304-5 (ebk); ISBN 978-1-119-48300-7 (ebk);
ISBN 978-1-119-48299-4 (Part 1); ISBN 978-1-119-48303-8 (Part 3)

Printed in the United States of America
10 9 8 7 6 5 4 3 2 1

Contents

Preface

The Wiley CIAexcel Exam Review Focus Notes 2018 are developed for each of the three parts of the Certified Internal Auditor (CIA) exam sponsored by the Institute of Internal Auditors (IIA). The purpose of the Focus Notes is to digest and assimilate the vast amounts of knowledge, skills, and abilities tested on the CIA exam in a clear, concise, easy-to-read, and easy-to-use format anywhere and any time to achieve success in the exam.

Each of the Focus Notes book topics is organized in the same way as the Wiley CIAexcel Exam Review book topics, that is, one Focus Notes book for each of the three-part review books. This clear linkage makes the exam study time more efficient and long-lasting, and provides the ability to recall important concepts, tools, and techniques, and the IIA Standards tested on the CIA exams. The Focus Notes can be used with any other study materials that you have determined works best for you to prepare for the CIA Exam. The Focus Notes provide a quick and easy refresher to the material that you are studying.

The Wiley Focus Notes are similar to index cards and flash cards in terms of purpose. The Focus Notes complement and supplement, not substitute, the Wiley Review books, where the former provides a summarized theory and the latter provides a detailed theory.

For those students who are exclusively studying the Wiley's preparation resources, we sincerely recommend the CIA Exam candidate to study the Focus Notes and Glossary section for each part just a few weeks before taking the actual exam for maximum retention and recall of the subject matter, assuming that the candidate has previously studied the Wiley CIAexcel Exam Review books.

The Focus Notes books will be especially useful to auditors who are traveling on an audit assignment, as well as others who are not traveling, due to their small and compact size, giving portability. The simplified summaries included in this material will help you learn the essential knowledge as well as help you retain them for years to come. The Focus Notes book can also be used as a desk reference on a post-exam basis, similar to a dictionary.

CIA Exam Study Preparation Resources

We recommend the following study plan and three review products for each Part of the CIA Exam to succeed in the exam:

- Read each part's review book (Theory)

- Practice the web-based online test bank software (Practice)

- Reinforce the theoretical concepts by studying the Focus Notes (Theory)

A series of **review books** have been prepared for the candidate to utilize for all three parts of the new CIA exam. Each part's review book includes a comprehensive coverage of the subject matter (theory) followed by some sample practice multiple-choice (M/C) questions with answers and explanations (practice). The sample practice M/C questions included in the review book are taken from the Wiley's web-based online test software to show you the flavor of questions. Each part's review book contains a glossary section, which is a good source for answering M/C questions on the CIA Exam.

The **web-based online test bank software** is a robust review product that simulates the format of the actual CIA Exam in terms of look and feel, thus providing intense practice and greater confidence to the CIA Exam candidates. The thousands of sample practice questions (5,275 plus) included in the online test bank can provide greater confidence and solid assurance to CIA exam candidates in that they are preparing well for all the required topics tested in the exam. All practice questions include explanations for the correct answer and are organized by domain topics within each part. Visit www.wileycia.com.

The following is a part summary showing the number of sample practice questions included in the online test bank and the number of questions tested in the actual CIA Exam.

Part Summary	Wiley Sample Practice Questions	CIA Exam Actual Test Questions
Part 1	750+	125
Part 2	725+	100
Part 3	3,800+	100
Total Questions in Three Parts	**5,275+**	**325**

Focus Notes provide a quick review and reinforcement of the important theoretical concepts, which are presented in a summary manner taken from the details of the review books. The Focus Notes can be studied just before the exam, during travel time, or any other time available to the student.

When combined, these three review products provide a great value to CIA Exam students and we are positive that they will recognize the value when they see it, feel it, and experience it.

We suggest a sequential study approach in four steps for each part of the exam, as follows:

Step 1. Read the glossary section at the end of each part's review book for a better understanding of key technical terms

Step 2. Study the theory from the each part's review book

Step 3. Practice the multiple-choice questions from the online test bank for each part

Step 4. Read the Focus Notes for each part for a quick review and reinforcement of the important theoretical concepts

In addition, the CIA Exam candidates should read **Practice Guides** from the IIA because these guides provide detailed guidance for conducting internal audit activities. They include detailed processes and procedures, such as tools and techniques, audit work programs, and step-by-step audit approaches, as well as examples of audit deliverables. These Practice Guides are not included in the Wiley Review Books due to their voluminous size and the fact that they are available from www.theiia.org.

CIA Exam-Taking Tips and Techniques

The types of questions a candidate can expect to see in the CIA Exam are objective and scenario-based multiple-choice (M/C) questions. Answering the M/C questions requires a good amount of practice and effort. The following tips and techniques will be helpful in answering the CIA Exam questions:

- Stay with your first impression of the correct choice.

- Know the subject area or topic. Don't read too much into the question.

- Remember that questions are independent of specific country, products, practices, vendors, hardware, software, or industry.

- Read the last sentence of the question first followed by all choices and then the body (stem) of the question.

- Read the question twice or read the underlined or circled keywords twice, and watch for tip-off words, such as **not, except, all, every, always, never, least,** or **most**, which denote absolute conditions.

- Do not project the question into your organizational environment, practices, policies, procedures, standards, and guidelines. The examination is focusing on the IIA's Professional Standards and Publications and on the CIA's exam syllabus (i.e., content specifications).

- Try to eliminate wrong choices as quickly as possible. When you get down to two semifinal choices, take a big-picture approach. For example, if choice A and D are the semifinalists, and choice D could be a part of choice A, then select choice A; or if choice D could be a more complete answer, then select choice D.

- Don't spend too much time on one question. If you are not sure of an answer, move on, and go back to it if time permits. The last resort is to guess the answer. There is no penalty for guessing the wrong answer.

Remember that success in any professional examination depends on several factors required of any student such as time management skills, preparation time and effort levels, education and experience levels, memory recall of the subject matter, state of the mind before or during the exam, and decision-making skills.

CIA Exam Content Specifications

Part 2 of the CIA Exam is called Internal Audit Practice and the exam duration is 2.0 hours (120 minutes) with 100 multiple-choice questions. The following is a breakdown of topics in Part 2.

Domain I: Managing the Internal Audit Function (40–50%)*

A. Strategic role of internal audit

- Initiate, manage, be a change catalyst, and cope with change (P)**

- Build and maintain networking with other organization executives and the audit committee (P)

- Organize and lead a team in mapping, analysis, and business process improvement (P)

- Assess and foster the ethical climate of the board and management (P)

- Educate senior management and the board on best practices in governance, risk management, control, and compliance (P)

---

*Indicates the relative range of weights assigned to this topic area for both theory and practice sections in the CIA Exam.

**Indicates the level of difficulty for each topic in the CIA Exam expressed as (A) for Awareness and (P) for Proficiency. (A) = Candidates must exhibit awareness (i.e., knowledge of terminology and fundamentals) in these topic areas. (P) = Candidates must exhibit proficiency (i.e., thorough understanding and ability to apply concepts) in these topic areas.

- Communicate internal audit key performance indicators to senior management and the board on a regular basis (P)

- Coordinate internal audit efforts with external auditor, regulatory oversight bodies, and other internal assurance functions (P)

B. Operational role of internal audit

- Formulate policies and procedures for the planning, organizing, directing, and monitoring of internal audit operations (P)

- Review the role of the internal audit function within the risk management framework (P)

- Direct administrative activities (e.g., budgeting and human resources) of the internal audit department (P)

- Interview candidates for internal audit positions (P)

- Report on the effectiveness of corporate risk management processes to senior management and the board (P)

- Report on the effectiveness of the internal control and risk management frameworks (P)

- Maintain an effective Quality Assurance Improvement program (P)

C. Establish risk-based internal audit plan

- Use market, product, and industry knowledge to identify new internal audit engagement opportunities (P)

- Use a risk framework to identify sources of potential engagements (e.g., audit universe, audit cycle requirements, management requests, and regulatory mandates) (P)

- Establish a framework for assessing risk (P)

- Rank and validate risk priorities to prioritize engagements in the audit plan (P)

- Identify internal audit resource requirements for annual internal audit plan (P)

- Communicate areas of significant risk and obtain approval from the board for the annual engagement plan (P)

Domain II: Managing Individual Engagements (40–50%)

A. Plan engagements

- Establish engagement objectives/criteria and finalize the scope of the engagement (P)

- Plan engagements to assure identification of key risks and controls (P)

- Complete a detailed risk assessment of each audit area (i.e., prioritize or evaluate risk and control factors) (P)

- Determine engagement procedures and prepare engagement work program (P)

- Determine the level of staff and resources needed for the engagement (P)

- Construct audit staff schedule for effective use of time (P)

B. Supervise Engagement

- Direct or supervise individual engagements (P)

- Nurture instrumental relations, build bonds, and work with others toward shared goals (P)

- Coordinate work assignments among audit team members when serving as the auditor-in-charge of a project (P)

- Review work papers (P)

- Conduct exit conference (P)

- Complete performance appraisals of engagement staff (P)

C. Communicate Engagement Results

- Initiate preliminary communication with engagement clients (P)

- Communicate interim progress (P)

- Develop recommendations when appropriate (P)

- Prepare report or other communication (P)

- Approve engagement report (P)

- Determine distribution of the report (P)

- Obtain management response to the report (P)

- Report outcomes to appropriate parties (P)

D. Monitor Engagement Outcomes

- Identify appropriate method to monitor engagement outcomes (P)

- Monitor engagement outcomes and conduct appropriate follow-up by the internal audit activity (P)

- Conduct follow-up and report on management's responses to internal audit recommendations (P)

- Report significant audit issues to senior management and the board periodically (P)

Domain III: Fraud Risks and Controls (5–15%)

A. Consider the potential for fraud risks and identify common types of fraud associated with the engagement area during the engagement planning process (P)

B. Determine if fraud risks require special consideration when conducting an engagement (P)

C. Determine if any suspected fraud merits investigation (P)

D. Complete a process review to improve controls to prevent fraud and recommend changes (P)

E. Employ audit tests to detect fraud (P)

F. Support a culture of fraud awareness and encourage the reporting of improprieties (P)

G. Interrogation or investigative techniques (A)

H. Forensic auditing (A)

STRATEGIC ROLE OF INTERNAL AUDIT

Managing the Internal Audit Department

The internal audit director needs to comply with the IIA's **Attribute Standards and Performance Standards**, which say that the chief audit executive (CAE) is responsible for properly managing the department so that: (1) audit work fulfills the general purposes and responsibilities approved by senior management and accepted by the board, (2) resources of the internal auditing (IA) department are efficiently and effectively employed, and (3) audit work conforms to these **Standards**.

Internal Audit Charter

- Basic policy statement under which the internal auditing (IA) department operates.

- Establishes the IA department's position in the organization's hierarchy.

- IA department operates independently of all other departments in the organization.

- Describes the organizational status that the director of internal auditing should report to the chief executive officer (CEO) but have access to the board of directors. A dual reporting relationship exists here: reporting administratively to the president or CEO, and reporting functionally to the audit committee of the board of directors.

- Describes the purpose, authority, and responsibility of the IA department.

Mission or Purpose of the IA Department

- Review organization's activities to determine whether it is efficiently and effectively carrying out its function of controlling in accordance with management's instructions, policies, and procedures.

- Determine the adequacy and effectiveness of the system of internal controls in all areas of activity.

- Review the reliability and integrity of financial information and the means used to identify, measure, classify, and report such information.

- Review the means of safeguarding assets and, as appropriate, verify the existence of such assets.

- Appraise the economy and efficiency with which resources are employed, identify opportunities to improve operating performance, and recommend solutions to problems where appropriate.

- Review operations and plans to ascertain whether results are consistent with established objectives and goals, and whether the operations and plans are being carried out as intended.

- Coordinate audit efforts, where appropriate, with those of the external auditors.

Mission or Purpose of the IA Department (continued)

- Review the planning, design, development, implementation, and operation of relevant computer-based systems to determine whether (a) adequate controls are incorporated in the systems; (b) thorough system testing is performed at appropriate stages; (c) system documentation is complete and accurate; and (d) needs of the users are met.

- Conduct periodic audits of computer centers and make post-installation evaluations of relevant data processing systems to determine whether those systems meet their intended purposes and objectives.

- Participate in the planning and performance of audits of acquisitions. Follow up to ensure the proper accomplishment of the audit objective.

- Report to those members of management who should be informed, or who should take corrective action, the results of audit examinations, the audit opinions formed, and the recommendations made.

- Evaluate the plans or actions taken to correct reported conditions for satisfactory disposition of audit findings. If corrective action is considered unsatisfactory, hold further discussions to achieve acceptable disposition.

- Provide adequate follow-up to ensure that proper corrective action is taken and that it is effective.

Authority

- The IA department will have full, free, and unrestricted access to records, personnel, and physical properties relevant to the performance of an audit.

- Internal auditors have neither authority over nor responsibility for the activities they audit.

- Audit director should have direct access to the audit committee since it tends to enhance IA's independence and objectivity.

Responsibility

The IA department accomplishes its purpose of assisting management by reviewing, examining, and evaluating activities, furnishing analyses and appraisals, and reporting findings and recommendations. This audit responsibility cannot relieve any operating manager of the requirement for ensuring proper control within his or her area of concern.

The IA department also has the responsibility to perform audit work with due professional care and with appropriate education, experience, certification, professional image and attitude, and personal integrity.

Nature of Work

- The scope of internal auditing work encompasses a systematic, disciplined approach to evaluating and improving the *adequacy* and *effectiveness* of risk management, control, and governance processes and the quality of performance in carrying out assigned responsibilities.

- *Adequacy* of risk management, control, and governance processes is present if management has planned and designed processes in a manner that provides reasonable assurance that the organization's objectives and goals will be achieved efficiently and economically.

- *Effectiveness* of risk management, control, and governance processes is present if management directs processes in such a manner as to provide reasonable assurance that the organization's objectives and goals will be achieved.

- The primary objectives of the overall management process are to achieve: relevant, reliable, and credible financial and operating information; effective and efficient use of the organization's resources; safeguarding of the organization's assets; compliance with laws, regulations, ethical and business norms, and contracts; identification of risk exposures and use of effective strategies to control them; established objectives and goals for operations or programs.

Nature of Work (continued)

- *Control* is any action taken by management to enhance the likelihood that established objectives and goals will be achieved.

- All business systems, processes, operations, functions, and activities within the organization are subject to the internal auditors' evaluations. The comprehensive scope of work of internal auditing should provide reasonable assurance that management's risk management system is effective; system of internal control is adequate, effective, and efficient; and governance process is effective by establishing and preserving values, setting goals, monitoring activities and performance, and defining the measures of accountability.

Auditor's Role in Quarterly Financial Reporting, Disclosures, and Management Certifications

Internal auditors should consider the following guidance regarding quarterly financial reports, disclosures, and management certifications related to requirements of the Securities and Exchange Commission (SEC) applicable to both U.S. registrants and foreign registrants.

- The strength of all financial markets depends on investor confidence. Events involving allegations of misdeeds by corporate executives, independent auditors, and other market participants have undermined that confidence. In response to this threat, U.S. legislative bodies and regulatory agencies in other countries passed legislation and regulations affecting corporate disclosures and financial reporting (e.g., in the United States, the Sarbanes-Oxley Act of 2002 required additional disclosures and certifications of financial statements by principal executive and financial officers).

- The new law challenges companies to devise processes that will permit senior officers to acquire the necessary assurances on which to base their personal certification. A key component of the certification process is the management of risk and internal controls over the recording and summarizing of financial information.

Statutory Requirements

Section 302 of the Sarbanes-Oxley Act outlines the corporate responsibility for financial reports, and the Securities and Exchange Commission (SEC) has issued guidance to implement the Act. As adopted, SEC Rules 13a-14 and 15d-14 require an issuer's principal executive officer(s) and the principal financial officer(s), or persons performing similar functions, to certify in each quarterly and annual report, including transition reports, filed or submitted by the issuer under Section 13(a) or 15(d) of the SEC's Exchange Act, that they have complied with the Act.

Recommended Actions

- The internal auditor's role in such processes may range from initial designer of the process, participant on a disclosure committee, or coordinator or liaison between management and its auditors, to independent assessor of the process.

- All internal auditors involved in quarterly reporting and disclosure processes should have a clearly defined role and evaluate responsibilities with appropriate IIA *Consulting and Assurance Standards* and with guidance contained in related Practice Advisories.

- Internal auditors should ensure that organizations have a formal policy and documented procedures to govern processes for quarterly financial reports, related disclosures, and regulatory reporting requirements.

- Internal auditors should encourage organizations to establish a "disclosure committee" to coordinate the process and provide oversight to participants. Representatives from key areas of the organization should be represented on the committee.

- Internal auditors should periodically review and evaluate quarterly reporting and disclosure processes, disclosure committee activities, and related documentation, and provide management and the audit committee with an assessment of the process and assurance concerning overall operations and compliance with policies and procedures.

Recommended Actions (continued)

- Internal auditors should recommend appropriate improvements to the policies, procedures, and process for quarterly reporting and related disclosures based on the results of an assessment of related activities.

- Internal auditors should compare processes for complying with Section 302 of the Sarbanes-Oxley Act (quarterly financial reporting and disclosures) to procedures developed to comply with Section 404 concerning management's annual assessment and public report on internal controls. Processes designed to be similar or compatible will contribute to operational efficiencies and reduce the likelihood or risk for problems and errors to occur or go undetected.

Auditing the Financial Reporting Process

- Executive management is the owner of the control environment and financial information, including the notes accompanying the financial statements and the accompanying disclosures in the financial report.

- The external auditor assures the financial report user that the reported information fairly presents the financial condition and result of operations of the organization in accordance with generally accepted accounting principles.

- The internal auditor performs procedures to provide a level of assurance to senior management and the audit or other committee of the governing board that controls surrounding the processes supporting the development of financial reports are effective.

Reporting on Internal Control

- An organization's audit or other board committee and internal auditing activity have interlocking goals. The core role of the CAE is to ensure that the audit committee receives the support and assurance services it needs and requests.

- Internal audit activity's work plans and specific assurance engagements begin with a careful identification of the exposures facing the organization, and internal audit's work plan is based on the risks and the assessment of the risk management and controls processes maintained by management to mitigate those risks.

A Framework for Internal Control

- Several widely accepted control models exist to assess the internal control system of an organization (e.g., COSO and CoCo). Any other recognized and credible model is appropriate to use.

- The COSO model states:

  - Internal control is not limited to accounting controls and is not narrowly restricted to financial reporting.

  - While accounting and financial reports are important issues, there are other important factors such as resource protection, operational efficiency and effectiveness, and compliance with rules, regulations, and organization policies that impact the financial reporting.

  - Internal control is management's responsibility and requires the participation of all persons within an organization, if it is to be effective.

  - The control framework is tied to the business objectives and is flexible enough to be adaptable.

Reporting on the Effectiveness of Internal Control

- The CAE should provide to the audit committee the internal audit's assessment of the effectiveness of the organization's system of controls, including its judgment on the adequacy of the control model or design. A governing board must rely on management to maintain an adequate and effective internal control system. It will reinforce that reliance with independent oversight.

- Internal controls cannot ensure success. Bad decisions, poor managers, or environmental factors can negate controls. Also, dishonest management may override controls and ignore or stifle communications from subordinates.

Roles for the Internal Auditor

- The CAE needs to review internal audit's risk assessment and audit plans for the year, if adequate resources have not been committed to helping senior management, the audit committee, and the external auditor with their responsibilities in the upcoming year's financial reporting regimentation.

- The CAE should allocate the internal audit's resources to the financial reporting, governance, and control processes consistent with the organization's risk assessment. The CAE should perform procedures that provide a level of assurance to senior management and the audit committee that controls surrounding the processes supporting the development of financial reports are adequately designed and effectively executed.

- Topics that the CAE may consider in supporting the organization's governance process and the oversight responsibilities of the governing board and its audit committee (or other designated committee) to ensure the reliability and integrity of financial reports should include financial reporting, corporate governance, and corporate control.

Control Criteria

- Before controls can be evaluated, management should determine the level of risk they want to take in the area to be reviewed. Internal auditors should identify what that level of risk is.

- If management has not identified the key risks and the level of risk they want to take, the internal audit may be able to help them through the facilitation of risk identification workshops or other techniques used by the organization.

- Once the risk level is determined, the controls currently in place can be assessed to determine how successful they are expected to be in reducing the risk to the desired level.

Corporate Governance Definition

Corporate governance refers to the method by which a firm is being governed, directed, administered, or controlled and to the goals for which it is being governed. It is concerned with the relative roles, rights, and accountability of such stakeholder groups as owners, boards of directors, managers, employees, and others who assert to be stakeholders.

Corporate Governance Principles and Issues

- Principles and components of corporate governance. (Four components include shareholders, board of directors, management, and employees.)

- Separation of ownership from control.

- Role of the board of directors.

- Need for board independence.

- Issues surrounding compensation: Major issues include CEO compensation (e.g., salaries, bonuses, stock options, and perks) and outside director compensation.

- Consequences of merger, acquisition, and takeover wave and divestiture of assets.

- Insider trading scandals.

- Board member liability.

- Lack of strong voice for board of directors due to their submissive behaviors.

- Improving corporate governance: (1) changes in boards of directors to include more outside directors and (2) increased role of shareholders in the governance process.

Role of the Internal Audit Activity and Internal Auditor in the Ethical Culture of an Organization

Governance and Organizational Culture

The way in which an organization chooses to conduct its affairs to meet the following four responsibilities: (1) Complies with society's legal and regulatory rules, (2) Satisfies the generally accepted business norms, ethical precepts, and social expectations of society, (3) Provides overall benefit to society and enhances the interests of the specific stakeholders in both the long term and the short term, and (4) Reports fully and truthfully to its owners, regulators, other stakeholders, and general public to ensure accountability for its decisions, actions, conduct, and performance is commonly referred to as its *governance process*. The organization's governing body and its senior management are accountable for the effectiveness of the governance process.

Shared Responsibility for the Organization's Ethical Culture

All people associated with the organization share some responsibility for the state of its ethical culture. Because of the complexity and dispersion of decision-making processes in most enterprises, each individual should be encouraged to be an ethics advocate, whether the role is delegated officially or merely conveyed informally. Codes of conduct and statements of vision and policy are important declarations of the organization's values and goals, the behavior expected of its people, and the strategies for maintaining a culture that aligns with its legal, ethical, and societal responsibilities.

Internal Audit Activity as Ethics Advocate

- Internal auditors and the internal audit activity should take an active role in support of the organization's ethical culture.

- The internal audit activity may assume one of several different roles as an ethics advocate. Those roles include chief ethics officer (ombudsman, compliance officer, management ethics counselor, or ethics expert), member of an internal ethics council, or assessor of the organization's ethical climate. In some circumstances, the role of chief ethics officer may conflict with the independence attribute of the internal audit activity.

Assessment of the Organization's Ethical Climate

At a minimum, the internal audit activity should periodically assess the state of the ethical climate of the organization and the effectiveness of its strategies, tactics, communications, and other processes in achieving the desired level of legal and ethical compliance.

Role of Corporate Code of Ethics

Ethics is knowing what is right or wrong, proper or improper. Ethics forms basic ground rules for individuals to follow.

Corporate Culture versus Corporate Ethics

Corporate culture is identified formally in written statements of corporate vision or mission statements, or as a set of basic qualities, values, beliefs, or commitments.

Corporate culture raises the overall sense of ethical behavior in a way that is easy to understand and accept. Corporate culture needs to include the ethical element.

A good corporate culture should incorporate a substantial part of corporate ethics, explicitly or implicitly.

Conflict of Interest

The conflict-of-interest policy often is considered a part of the overall ethics policies. Conflict-of-interest concerns sometimes constitute the main part of ethics standards.

Factors Influencing Ethical Standards

Factors causing *higher* ethical standards:

- Public disclosure, publicity, media coverage, and better communication

- Increased public concern, public awareness, consciousness and security, better-informed public, and societal pressures

- Government regulation, legislation and intervention, and federal courts

- Education of business managers, increase in manager professionalism, and education

- New social expectation of the role that business is to play in society and the attitudes of young adults

- Greater sense of social responsibility on the part of organizations and greater awareness of the implications of their actions

- Business responsiveness, corporate policy changes, and top management's emphasis on ethical action

  Factors causing *lower* ethical standards:

- Society's lower standards, social decay, more permissive society, growth of materialism and hedonism, loss of church and home influence, and less quality, more quantity desires

Factors Influencing Ethical Standards (continued)

- Competition, pace of life, the stress of trying to succeed, current economic conditions, and the cost of doing business

- Political corruption, loss of confidence in government, politics, political ethics, and climate

- People being more aware of unethical acts, constant media coverage, and communications that create an atmosphere for crime

- Greed, desire for gain, worship of the dollar as a measure of success, selfishness, and a lack of personal integrity and moral fiber

- Pressure for profit from within the organization from superiors or stockholders, corporate influences on managers, and corporate policies

It is easy to rationalize unethical conduct in business because of the prevailing theory that executives must provide stockholders with the greatest possible return on their investments (i.e., profit). This leads us to believe that ethical practices are rarely rewarded when compared to profits.

Options for Facilitating Ethical Behavior

• Distributing the code in a training program with top management attendance

• Transmitting the code with the chief executive officer's personal letter (tone-from-the-top)

• Showing ethics examples in a workshop (role-playing)

• Showing videotapes with top management supportive comments

Monitoring Compliance with the Code of Conduct

Compliance with the code of conduct is an ongoing responsibility of each employee and is primarily based on the honor system. Employees should be asked to certify or sign a form asserting that they have complied with the code or to list exceptions to such compliance.

Tools to Monitor Compliance

- Annual survey
- Periodic query
- Ethics review board
- Policy guidance
- Employee indoctrination
- Periodic review by internal audit

Fraud in Financial Reporting

The Treadway Commission in 1987 made specific recommendations on the Code of Corporate Conduct, as follows: The public company should develop and enforce written codes of corporate conduct. Codes of conduct should foster a strong ethical climate and open channels of communication to help protect against fraudulent financial reporting. As a part of its ongoing oversight of the effectiveness of internal controls, a company's audit committee should annually review the program that management establishes to monitor compliance with the code.

Activities to Ensure a Standing Level of Conduct

- Proper hiring practices
- Competitive levels of compensation
- Performance incentives
- Company tradition and reputation
- Control mechanisms
- Proper organization structure

Fraud in Financial Reporting (continued)

Business Practices that Constitute Areas of Ethical Dilemma

- Hidden defects in products and poor services
- Unfair credit practices
- Deceptive advertising
- Overselling of products and services
- Overcharging of customers and clients
- Unreal delivery dates for products and services
- Products that are unhealthy and dangerous, causing injury to people

Example of the Content of a Code of Conduct

Although each organization is different in some respects, certain types of employee behavior can be expected in all organizations. The contents of a code of conduct are divided into three groups: (1) mandatory (those items that should always appear in a code-of-conduct document), (2) strongly suggested, and (3) desirable. Factors that determine what is appropriate for each specific code are based on a complete understanding of the business and corporate culture.

Ethics Implementation Procedures

- Ethics committee
- Hotline phone
- Counsel for guidance
- Compliance review board
- Internal complaint and appeal mechanism
- Ombudsman

Integrating Ethical Standards in Complex Situations

It is good to integrate ethical standards with company policies and procedures, conflict-of-interest statements, job/position descriptions, employee performance evaluations, vision/mission statements, posters and marketing/advertising materials, product packing materials, management employment contracts, legal contracts with outsiders, purchase orders and invoices, employment/job applications, and company annual reports.

Ethics-related statements should be included in so many places for reinforcement purposes and because not everyone will have access to the same ethics-related materials. For example, a consultant may not have access to job descriptions and employee performance evaluations that an employee would have. Similarly, outsiders, such as investors and creditors, would have more access to a company's annual report than to a company policy manual or job application or description.

Another way to integrate ethical standards in complex situations is to measure a manager's performance based on both quantitative and qualitative factors. Usually managers' bonuses or other rewards are based on how well they meet their quantitative goals, such as increase in revenues or decrease in costs. While these goals are good, managers should also be measured on qualitative factors, such as: quality; working relations with customers, suppliers, and employees; and productivity levels.

An organization's goals are interrelated. This fact should be considered during the establishment and evaluation of individual manager's goals and actual performance.

Integrating Ethical Standards in Complex Situations (continued)

By placing emphasis on only one or a few goals, the other related goals may be in jeopardy. For example, focusing on increasing revenues or decreasing costs alone is not enough because these goals might have been achieved by jeopardizing or manipulating other related goals, such as too much inventory or too little inventory, or too much maintenance expense or too little maintenance expense, or expensing fixed asset acquisitions instead of capitalizing.

IIA *STANDARDS* APPLICABLE TO STRATEGIC ROLE OF INTERNAL AUDIT

Direct Interaction with the Board

The chief audit executive (CAE) must communicate and interact directly with the board (IIA Standard 1111).

1. Direct communication occurs when the CAE regularly attends and participates in board meetings that relate to the board's oversight responsibilities for auditing, financial reporting, organizational governance, and control. The CAE's attendance and participation at these meetings provide an opportunity to be apprised of strategic business and operational developments and to raise high-level risk, systems, procedures, or control issues at an early stage. Meeting attendance also provides an opportunity to exchange information concerning the internal audit activity's plans and activities and to keep each other informed on any other matters of mutual interest.

2. Such communication and interaction also occurs when the CAE meets privately with the board, at least annually.

Managing the Internal Audit Activity

The CAE must manage the internal audit activity effectively to ensure it adds value to the organization (IIA Standard 2000).

The internal audit activity is effectively managed when:

- The results of the internal audit activity's work achieve the purpose and responsibility included in the internal audit charter.

- The internal audit activity conforms with the definition of internal auditing and the *Standards*.

- The individuals who are part of the internal audit activity demonstrate conformance with the Code of Ethics and the *Standards*.

The internal audit activity adds value to the organization (and its stakeholders) when it provides objective and relevant assurance and contributes to the effectiveness and efficiency of governance, risk management, and control processes.

Communication and Approval

The CAE must communicate the internal audit activity's plans and resource requirements, including significant interim changes, to senior management and the board for review and approval. The CAE must also communicate the impact of resource limitations (IIA Standard 2020).

1. The CAE will submit annually to senior management and the board for review and approval a summary of the internal audit plan, work schedule, staffing plan, and financial budget. This summary will inform senior management and the board of the scope of internal audit work and of any limitations placed on that scope. The CAE will also submit all significant interim changes for approval and information.

2. The approved engagement work schedule, staffing plan, and financial budget, along with all significant interim changes, are to contain sufficient information to enable senior management and the board to ascertain whether the internal audit activity's objectives and plans support those of the organization and the board and are consistent with the internal audit charter.

Policies and Procedures

The CAE must establish policies and procedures to guide the internal audit activity. The form and content of policies and procedures are dependent on the size and structure of the internal audit activity and the complexity of its work (IIA Standard 2040).

The CAE develops policies and procedures. Formal administrative and technical audit manuals may not be needed by all internal audit activities. A small internal audit activity may be managed informally. Its audit staff may be directed and controlled through daily, close supervision and memoranda that state policies and procedures to be followed. In a large internal audit activity, more formal and comprehensive policies and procedures are essential to guide the internal audit staff in the execution of the internal audit plan.

Nature of Work

The internal audit activity must evaluate and contribute to the improvement of governance, risk management, and control processes using a systematic and disciplined approach (IIA Standard 2100).

Governance

The internal audit activity must assess and make appropriate recommendations for improving the governance process in its accomplishment of these objectives:

- Promoting appropriate ethics and values within the organization

- Ensuring effective organizational performance management and accountability

- Communicating risk and control information to appropriate areas of the organization

- Coordinating the activities of and communicating information among the board, external and internal auditors, and management

The internal audit activity must evaluate the design, implementation, and effectiveness of the organization's ethics-related objectives, programs, and activities.

The internal audit activity must assess whether the information technology (IT) governance of the organization supports the organization's strategies and objectives (IIA Standard 2110).

Governance Definition

1. The role of internal auditing as noted in the definition of internal auditing includes the responsibility to evaluate and improve governance processes as part of the assurance function.

2. The term "governance" has a range of definitions depending on a variety of environmental, structural, and cultural circumstances, as well as legal frameworks. The *International Standards for the Professional Practice of Internal Auditing* (*Standards*) define "governance" as "the combination of processes and structures implemented by the board to inform, direct, manage, and monitor the activities of the organization toward the achievement of its objectives." The CAE may use a different definition for audit purposes when the organization has adopted a different governance framework or model.

3. Globally, a variety of governance models that have been published by other organizations and legal and regulatory bodies. For example, the Organisation for Economic Co-operation and Development (OECD) defines "governance" as "a set of relationships between a company's management, its board, its shareholders, and other stakeholders. Corporate governance provides the structure through which the objectives of the company are set and the means of attaining those objectives and monitoring performance are determined." The Australian Securities Exchange Corporate Governance Council defines "governance" as "the system by which companies are directed and managed. It influences how the objectives of the company are set and achieved, how risk is monitored and assessed, and how performance is optimized." In most instances, there is

Governance Definition (continued)

an indication that governance is a process or system and is not static. What distinguishes the approach in the *Standards* is the specific emphasis on the board and its governance activities.

4. The frameworks and requirements for governance vary according to organization type and regulatory jurisdictions. Examples include publicly traded companies, not-for-profit organizations, associations, government or quasi-government entities, academic institutions, private companies, commissions, and stock exchanges.

5. How an organization designs and practices the principles of effective governance also vary depending on the size, complexity, and life cycle maturity of the organization, its stakeholder structure, legal and cultural requirements, and so on.

6. As a consequence of the variation in the design and structure of governance, the CAE should work with the board and the executive management team, as appropriate, to determine how governance should be defined for audit purposes.

7. Internal auditing is integral to the organization's governance framework. Their unique position within the organization enables internal auditors to observe and formally assess the governance structure, its design, and its operational effectiveness while remaining independent.

8. The relationship among governance, risk management, and internal control should be considered. This item is addressed in Practice Advisory 2110-2. Practice Advisory 2110-3 discusses assessing governance.

Governance Relationship with Risk and Control

1. The *Standards* define "governance" as "the combination of processes and structures implemented by the board to inform, direct, manage, and monitor the activities of the organization toward the achievement of its objectives."

2. Governance does not exist as a set of distinct and separate processes and structures. Rather, there are relationships among governance, risk management, and internal controls.

3. Effective governance activities consider risk when setting strategy. Conversely, risk management relies on effective governance (e.g., tone at the top, risk appetite and tolerance, risk culture, and the oversight of risk management).

4. Effective governance relies on internal controls and communication to the board on the effectiveness of those controls.

5. Control and risk also are related, as "control" is defined as "any action taken by management, the board, and other parties to manage risk and increase the likelihood that established goals will be achieved."

Governance Relationship with Risk and Control (continued)

6. The CAE should consider these relationships in planning assessments of governance processes:

- An audit should address those controls in governance processes that are designed to prevent or detect events that could have a negative impact on the achievement of organizational strategies, goals, and objectives; operational efficiency and effectiveness; financial reporting; or compliance with applicable laws and regulations. (See Practice Advisory 2110-3.)

- Controls within governance processes are often significant in managing multiple risks across the organization. For example, controls around the code of conduct may be lied upon to manage compliance risks and fraud risks. This aggregation effect should be considered when developing the scope of an audit of governance processes.

- If other audits assess controls in governance processes (e.g., audits of controls over financial reporting, risk management processes, or compliance), the auditor should consider relying on the results of those audits.

Governance Assessments

1. Internal auditors can act in a number of different capacities in assessing and contributing to the improvement of governance practices. Typically, internal auditors provide independent, objective assessments of the design and operating effectiveness of the organization's governance processes. They also may provide consulting services and advice on ways to improve those processes. In some cases, internal auditors may be called on to facilitate board self-assessments of governance practices.

2. As noted in Practice Advisory 2110-1: *Governance: Definition*, the definition of governance for audit purposes should be agreed on with the board and executive management, as appropriate. In addition, the internal auditor should understand the organization's governance processes and the relationships among governance, risk, and control (refer to Practice Advisory 2110-2, *Governance: Relationship with Risk and Control*).

3. The audit plan should be developed based on an assessment of risks to the organization. All governance processes should be considered in the risk assessment. The plan should include the higher risk governance processes and an assessment of processes or risk areas where the board or executive management has requested work be performed should be considered. The plan should define the nature of the work to be performed, the governance processes to be addressed, and the nature of the assessments that will be made (i.e., macro— considering the entire governance framework, or micro—considering specific risks, processes, or activities, or some combination of both).

Governance Assessments (continued)

4. When there are known control issues or the governance process is not mature, the CAE could consider different methods for improving the control or governance processes through consulting services instead of, or in addition to, formal assessments.

5. Internal audit assessments regarding governance processes are likely to be based on information obtained from numerous audit assignments over time. The internal auditor should consider:

- The results of audits of specific governance processes (e.g., the whistleblower process, the strategy management process).

- Governance issues arising from audits that are not specifically focused on governance (e.g., audits of the risk management process, internal control over financial reporting, fraud risks).

- The results of other internal and external assurance providers' work (e.g., a firm engaged by the general counsel to review the investigation process). Refer to Practice Advisory 2050.

- Other information on governance issues, such as adverse incidents indicating an opportunity to improve governance processes.

Governance Assessments (continued)

6. During the planning, evaluating, and reporting phases, the internal auditor should be sensitive to the potential nature and ramifications of the results and ensure appropriate communications with the board and executive management. The internal auditor should consider consulting legal counsel both before initiating the audit and before finalizing the report.

7. The internal audit activity is an essential part of the governance process. The board and executive management should be able to rely on the quality assurance and improvement program (QAIP) of the internal audit activity in conjunction with external quality assessments performed in accordance with the *Standards* for assurance on its effectiveness.

Coordination

The CAE should share information and coordinate activities with other internal and external providers of assurance and consulting services to ensure proper coverage and minimize duplication of efforts (IIA Standard 2050).

Coordination Between External Auditors and Internal Auditors

1. Oversight of the work of external auditors, including coordination with the internal audit activity, is the responsibility of the board. Coordination of internal and external audit work is the responsibility of the CAE. The CAE obtains the support of the board to coordinate audit work effectively.

2. Organizations may use the work of external auditors to provide assurance related to activities within the scope of internal auditing. In these cases, the CAE takes the steps necessary to understand the work performed by the external auditors, including:

- The nature, extent, and timing of work planned by external auditors, to be satisfied that the external auditors' planned work, in conjunction with the internal auditors' planned work, satisfies the requirements of Standard 2100.

- The external auditor's assessment of risk and materiality.

- The external auditors' techniques, methods, and terminology to enable the CAE to:

  1. Coordinate internal and external auditing work.

  2. Evaluate, for purposes of reliance, the external auditors' work.

  3. Communicate effectively with external auditors.

Coordination Between External Auditors and Internal Auditors *(continued)*

- Access to the external auditors' programs and working papers, to be satisfied that the external auditors' work can be relied on for internal audit purposes. Internal auditors are responsible for respecting the confidentiality of those programs and working papers.

3. External auditors may rely on the work of the internal audit activity in performing their work. In this case, the CAE needs to provide sufficient information to enable external auditors to understand the internal auditors' techniques, methods, and terminology to facilitate reliance by external auditors on work performed. Access to the internal auditors' programs and working papers is provided to external auditors in order for external auditors to be satisfied as to the acceptability for external audit purposes of relying on the internal auditors' work.

4. It may be efficient for internal and external auditors to use similar techniques, methods, and terminology to coordinate their work effectively and to rely on the work of one another.

5. Planned audit activities of internal and external auditors need to be discussed to ensure that audit coverage is coordinated and duplicate efforts are minimized where possible. Sufficient meetings are to be scheduled during the audit process to ensure coordination of audit work and efficient and timely completion of audit activities and to determine whether observations and recommendations from work performed to date require that the scope of planned work be adjusted.

Coordination Between External Auditors and Internal Auditors (continued)

6. The internal audit activity's final communications, management's responses to those communications, and subsequent follow-up reviews are to be made available to external auditors. These communications assist external auditors in determining and adjusting the scope and timing of their work. In addition, internal auditors need access to the external auditors' presentation materials and management letters. Matters discussed in presentation materials and included in management letters need to be understood by the CAE and used as input to internal auditors in planning the areas to emphasize in future internal audit work. After review of management letters and initiation of any needed corrective action by appropriate members of senior management and the board, the CAE ensures that appropriate follow-up and corrective actions have been taken.

7. The CAE is responsible for regular evaluations of the coordination between internal and external auditors. Such evaluations may also include assessments of the overall efficiency and effectiveness of internal and external audit activities, including aggregate audit cost. The CAE communicates the results of these evaluations to senior management and the board, including relevant comments about the performance of external auditors.

Assurance Maps

1. One of the key responsibilities of the board is to gain assurance that processes are operating within the parameters it has established to achieve the defined objectives. It is necessary to determine whether risk management processes are working effectively and whether key or business-critical risks are being managed to an acceptable level.

2. Increased focus on the roles and responsibilities of senior management and boards has prompted many organizations to place a greater emphasis on assurance activities. The *Standards* Glossary defines assurance as "an objective examination of evidence for the purpose of providing an independent assessment on governance, risk management, and control processes for the organization." The board will use multiple sources to gain reliable assurance. Assurance from management is fundamental and should be complemented by the provision of objective assurance from internal audit and other third parties. Risk managers, internal auditors, and compliance practitioners are asking: Who does what and why? Boards in particular are beginning to question who is providing assurance, where is the delineation between the functions, and if there are any overlaps.

3. There are fundamentally three classes of assurance providers, differentiated by the stakeholders they serve, their level of independence from the activities over which they provide assurance, and the robustness of that assurance.

Assurance Maps (continued)

- Those who report to management and/or are part of management (management assurance), including individuals who perform control self-assessments, quality auditors, environmental auditors, and other management-designated assurance personnel

- Those who report to the board, including internal audit

- Those who report to external stakeholders (external audit assurance), which is a role traditionally fulfilled by the independent/statutory auditor

   4. There are many assurance providers for an organization.

- Line management and employees (management provides assurance as a first line of defense over the risks and controls for which they are responsible)

- Senior management

- Internal and external auditors

- Compliance

- Quality assurance

Assurance Maps (continued)

- Risk management

- Environmental auditors

- Workplace health and safety auditors

- Government performance auditors

- Financial reporting review teams

- Subcommittees of the board (e.g., audit, actuarial, credit, governance)

- External assurance providers, including surveys, specialist reviews (health and safety), and so on

5. The internal audit activity normally provides assurance over the entire organization, including risk management processes (both their design and operating effectiveness), management of those risks classified as key (including the effectiveness of the controls and other responses to them), verification of the reliability and appropriateness of the risk assessment, and reporting of the risk and control status.

6. With responsibility for assurance activities traditionally being shared among management, internal audit, risk management, and compliance, it is important that assurance activities be coordinated to ensure that

Assurance Maps (continued)

resources are used in the most efficient and effective way. Many organizations operate with traditional (and separate) internal audit, risk, and compliance activities. It is common for organizations to have a number of separate groups performing different risk management, compliance, and assurance functions independently of one another. Without effective coordination and reporting, work can be duplicated or key risks may be missed or misjudged.

7. While many organizations monitor the activities of internal audit, risk, and compliance, not all view all their activities in a holistic way. An assurance mapping exercise involves mapping assurance coverage against the key risks in an organization. This process allows an organization to identify and address any gaps in the risk management process and gives stakeholders comfort that risks are being managed and reported on and that regulatory and legal obligations are being met. Organizations will benefit from a streamlined approach, which ensures that the information is available to management about the risks they face and how the risks are being addressed. The mapping is done across the organization to understand where the overall risk and assurance roles and accountabilities reside. The aim is to ensure that there is a comprehensive risk and assurance process with no duplicated effort or potential gaps.

Assurance Maps (continued)

8. Often an organization will have defined the significant risk categories that make up its risk management framework. In such cases, the **assurance map** would be based on the structure of this framework. For example, an assurance map could have these columns:

- Significant risk category

- Management role responsible for the risk (risk owner)

- Inherent risk rating

- Residual risk rating

- External audit coverage

- Internal audit coverage

- Other assurance provider coverage

In this example, the CAE would populate the internal audit coverage column with recent coverage. Often each significant risk has a risk owner or a person responsible for coordinating assurance activities for that risk; if so, that person would populate the other assurance provider coverage column. Each significant unit within an

Assurance Maps (continued)

organization could have its own assurance map. Alternatively, the internal audit activity may play a coordinating role in developing and completing the organization's assurance map.

9. Once the assurance map for the organization has been completed, significant risks with inadequate assurance coverage, or areas of duplicated assurance coverage, can be identified. Senior management and the board need to consider changes in assurance coverage for these risks. The internal audit activity needs to consider areas of inadequate coverage when developing the internal audit plan.

10. It is the responsibility of the CAE to understand the independent assurance requirements of the board and the organization in order to clarify the role the internal audit activity fills and the level of assurance it provides. The board needs to be confident that the overall assurance process is adequate and sufficiently robust to validate that the risks of the organization are being managed and reported on effectively.

11. The board needs to receive information about assurance activities, both implemented and planned, in regard to each category of risk. The internal audit activity and other assurance providers offer the board the appropriate level of assurance for the nature and levels of risk that exist in the organization under the respective categories.

Assurance Maps (continued)

12. In organizations requiring an overall opinion from the CAE, the CAE needs to understand the nature, scope, and extent of the integrated assurance map to consider the work of other assurance providers (and rely on it as appropriate) before presenting an overall opinion on the organization's governance, risk management, and control processes. The IIA's *Practice Guide: Formulating and Expressing Internal Audit Opinions* provides additional guidance.

13. In instances where the organization does not expect an overall opinion, the CAE can act as the coordinator of assurance providers to ensure there are either no gaps in assurance, or the gaps are known and accepted. The CAE reports on any lack of input/involvement/ oversight/assurance over other assurance providers. If the CAE believes that the assurance coverage is inadequate or ineffective, senior management and the board need to be advised accordingly.

14. The CAE is directed by Standard 2050 to coordinate activities with other assurance providers; the use of an assurance map will help achieve this. Assurance maps increasingly offer an effective way of communicating this coordination.

Relying on the Work of Other Assurance Providers

1. The internal auditor may rely on or use the work of other internal or external assurance providers in providing governance, risk management, and control assurance to the board. Internal assurance providers could include company functions such as compliance, information security, quality, and labor health and safety as well as management monitoring activities. External assurance providers could include external auditors, joint venture partners, specialist reviews, or third-party audit firms, including those providing reports in accordance with International Standard on Assurance Engagements 3402, *Assurance Reports on Controls at a Service Organization*.

2. The decision to rely on the work of other assurance providers can be made for a variety of reasons, including to address areas that fall outside of the competence of the internal audit activity, to gain knowledge transfer from other assurance providers, or to efficiently enhance coverage of risk beyond the internal audit plan.

3. An internal audit charter and/or engagement letter should specify that the internal audit activity have access to the work of other internal and external assurance providers.

4. Where the internal auditor is hiring the assurance provider, the auditor should document engagement expectations in a contract or agreement. Minimum expectations should be provided for the nature and

Relying on the Work of Other Assurance Providers (continued)

ownership of deliverables, methods/techniques, the nature of procedures and data/information to be used, and progress reports/supervision to ensure the work is adequate and reporting requirements.

5. If management within the organization provides the contracting of, and direction to, a third-party assurance provider, the internal auditor should be satisfied that the instruction is appropriate, understood, and executed.

6. The internal auditor should consider the independence and objectivity of the other assurance providers when considering whether to rely on or use their work. If an assurance provider is hired by and/or is under the direction of management instead of internal auditing, the impact of this arrangement on the assurance provider's independence and objectivity should be evaluated.

7. The internal auditor should assess the competencies and qualifications of the provider performing the assurance work. Examples of competency include verifying the assurer holds appropriate professional experience and qualifications, has a current registration with the relevant professional body or institute, and has a reputation for competency and integrity in the sector.

8. The internal auditor should consider the other assurance provider's elements of practice to have reasonable assurance the findings are based on sufficient, reliable, relevant, and useful information, as required by

Relying on the Work of Other Assurance Providers (continued)

Standard 2310. *Identifying Information*. Standard 2310 must be met by the CAE regardless of the degree to which the work of other assurance providers is used.

9. The internal auditor should ensure that the work of the other assurance provider is appropriately planned, supervised, documented, and reviewed. The auditor should consider whether the audit evidence is appropriate and sufficient to determine the extent of use and reliance on the work of the other assurance providers. Based on an assessment of the work of the other assurance provider, additional work or test procedures may be needed to gain appropriate and sufficient audit evidence. The internal auditor should be satisfied, based on knowledge of the business, environment, techniques, and information used by the assurance provider, that the findings appear to be reasonable.

10. The level of reliance that can be placed on another assurance provider will be impacted by the factors mentioned earlier: independence, objectivity, competencies, elements of practice, adequacy of execution of audit work, and sufficiency of audit evidence to support the given level of assurance. As the risk or significance of the activity reviewed by the other assurance provider increases, the internal auditor should gather more information on these factors and may need to obtain additional audit evidence to supplement the work done by the other assurance provider. To increase the level of reliance on the results, the internal audit activity may retest results of the other assurance provider.

Relying on the Work of Other Assurance Providers (continued)

11. The internal auditor should incorporate the assurance provider's results into the overall report of assurance that the internal auditor reports to the board or other key stakeholders. Significant issues raised by the other assurance provider can be incorporated in detail or summarized in internal audit reports. The internal auditor should include reference to other assurance providers where reports rely on such information.

12. Follow-up is a process by which internal auditors evaluate the adequacy, effectiveness, and timeliness of actions taken by management on reported observations and recommendations, including those made by other assurance providers. In reviewing actions taken to address recommendations made by other assurance providers, the internal auditor should determine whether management has implemented the recommendations or assumed the risk of not implementing them.

13. Significant findings from other assurance providers should be considered in the assurance and communications internal auditing is providing the organization. In addition, results of work performed by others may impact the internal audit risk assessment as to whether the findings impact the evaluation of risk and the level of audit work necessary in response to that risk.

14. In evaluating the effectiveness of, and contributing to the improvement of, risk management processes (*Standard 2120*), the internal audit activity may review the processes of these internal assurance providers, including company functions such as compliance, information security, quality, and labor health and

Relying on the Work of Other Assurance Providers (continued)

safety as well as management monitoring activities. There should be coverage of risk areas by internal auditing, but when another assurance function exists, the internal audit activity may review the performance of that process rather than duplicate the detailed specific work of that other function.

15. Assessment from the other assurance provider on significant risks should be reported to relevant areas of the organization to be included in considerations regarding the organization's risk management framework and assurance map. See Practice Advisory 2050-2.

Reporting to Senior Management and the Board

The CAE must report periodically to senior management and the board on the internal audit activity's purpose, authority, responsibility, and performance relative to its plan. Reporting must also include significant risk exposures and control issues, including fraud risks, governance issues, and other matters needed or requested by senior management and the board (IIA Standard 2060).

The frequency and content of reporting are determined in discussion with senior management and the board and depend on the importance of the information to be communicated and the urgency of the related actions to be taken by senior management or the board.

Reporting to Senior Management and the Board (continued)

1. The purpose of reporting is to provide assurance to senior management and the board regarding governance processes (Standard 2110), risk management (Standard 2120), and control (Standard 2130). Standard 1111 states: "The CAE must communicate and interact directly with the board."

2. The CAE should agree with the board about the frequency and nature of reporting on the internal audit activity's charter (e.g., purpose, authority, and responsibility) and performance. Performance reporting should be relative to the most recently approved plan to inform senior management and the board of significant deviations from the approved audit plan, staffing plans, and financial budgets; reasons for the deviations; and action needed or taken. Standard 1320 states: "The chief audit executive must communicate the results of the quality assurance and improvement program to senior management and the board."

3. Significant risk exposures and control issues are those conditions that, according to the CAE's judgment, could adversely affect the organization and its ability to achieve its strategic, financial reporting, operational, and compliance objectives. Significant issues may carry unacceptable exposure to internal and external risks, including conditions related to control weaknesses, fraud, irregularities, illegal acts, errors, inefficiency, waste, ineffectiveness, conflicts of interest, and financial viability.

4. Senior management and the board make decisions on the appropriate action to be taken regarding significant issues. They may decide to assume the risk of not correcting the reported condition because of cost

Reporting to Senior Management and the Board (continued)

or other considerations. Senior management should inform the board of decisions about all significant issues raised by internal auditing.

5. When the CAE believes that senior management has accepted a level of risk that the organization considers unacceptable, the CAE must discuss the matter with senior management, as stated in Standard 2600. The CAE should understand management's basis for the decision, identify the cause of any disagreement, and determine whether management has the authority to accept the risk. Disagreements may relate to risk likelihood and potential exposure, understanding of risk appetite, cost, and level of control. Preferably, the CAE should resolve the disagreement with senior management.

6. If the CAE and senior management cannot reach an agreement, Standard 2600 directs the CAE to inform the board. If possible, the CAE and management should make a joint presentation about the conflicting positions. For financial reporting matters, CAEs should consider discussing these issues with the external auditors in a timely manner.

Risk Management

The internal audit activity must evaluate the effectiveness and contribute to the improvement of risk management processes (IIA Standard 2120).

Determining whether risk management processes are effective is a judgment resulting from the internal auditor's assessment that:

- Organizational objectives support and align with the organization's mission.

- Significant risks are identified and assessed.

- Appropriate risk responses are selected that align risks with the organization's risk appetite.

- Relevant risk information is captured and communicated in a timely manner across the organization, enabling staff, management, and the board to carry out their responsibilities.

The internal audit activity may gather the information to support this assessment during multiple engagements. The results of these engagements, when viewed together, provide an understanding of the organization's risk management processes and their effectiveness.

Risk management processes are monitored through ongoing management activities, separate evaluations, or both.

Risk Management (continued)

The internal audit activity must evaluate risk exposures relating to the organization's governance, operations, and information systems regarding the:

- Reliability and integrity of financial and operational information.

- Effectiveness and efficiency of operations and programs.

- Safeguarding of assets.

- Compliance with laws, regulations, policies, procedures, and contracts.

The internal audit activity must evaluate the potential for the occurrence of fraud and how the organization manages fraud risk.

During consulting engagements, internal auditors must address risk consistent with the engagement's objectives and be alert to the existence of other significant risks.

Internal auditors must incorporate knowledge of risks gained from consulting engagements into their evaluation of the organization's risk management processes.

When assisting management in establishing or improving risk management processes, internal auditors must refrain from assuming any management responsibility by actually managing risks.

Control

The internal audit activity must assist the organization in maintaining effective controls by evaluating their effectiveness and efficiency and by promoting continuous improvement (IIA Standard 2130).

The internal audit activity must evaluate the adequacy and effectiveness of controls in responding to risks within the organization's governance, operations, and information systems regarding the:

- Reliability and integrity of financial and operational information.

- Effectiveness and efficiency of operations and programs.

- Safeguarding of assets.

- Compliance with laws, regulations, policies, procedures, and contracts.

Internal auditors must incorporate knowledge of controls gained from consulting engagements into evaluation of the organization's control processes.

OPERATIONAL ROLE OF INTERNAL AUDIT

Planning

The director of internal auditing should establish plans to carry out the responsibilities of the internal auditing department. These plans should be consistent with the charter and with the goals for the organization. The planning process involves establishing goals, audit work schedules, staffing plans and financial budgets, and activity reports.

During audit planning, internal auditors should review all relevant information such as risk models/risk analysis, audit plans, audit assignments, and activity reports.

Risk Models/Risk Analysis

- Used in conjunction with development of long-range audit schedules.

- Judgment of the internal auditor and the results of quantitative risk assessment are the basis for audit planning work.

- Factors to be considered during risk analysis include:

  - Financial exposure

  - Potential loss of assets

  - Results of prior audits

  - Major operating changes

  - Damage to assets

  - Failure to comply with laws and regulations

Risk Models/Risk Analysis (continued)

- Skills available on the audit staff are not a risk factor since missing skills can be obtained elsewhere.

- The CAE should allocate the audit work schedule to managers based on risk analysis performed by auditors and skill analysis of the audit managers.

Audit Plan

The *audit plan* should include: a detailed schedule of areas to be audited during the coming year; an estimate of the time required for each audit, risk, exposure, and potential loss to the organization; and the approximate starting date for each audit.

Audit Assignment

Documentation needed to plan an audit assignment should include evidence that resources needed to complete the audit were considered. When the audit director makes audit assignments for inclusion in the work schedule, those assignments should be based on the relative risk of the auditable areas.

Criteria should be established when the audit resources are limited and a decision has to be made to choose between two operating departments for scheduling an audit. The most important criteria are: major changes in operations in one of the departments, more opportunities to achieve operating benefits in one of the departments than in the other, and when potential loss is significantly greater in one department than the other. Least important criteria are whether the audit staff has recently added an individual with experience in one of the auditable areas.

Activity Reports

Activity reports submitted periodically by the audit director to management and to the board should compare performance with audit work schedules. This requires comparing audits completed with audits planned.

Policies and Procedures

The CAE should provide written policies and procedures to guide the audit staff. An audit policies and procedures manual is most essential for guiding the audit staff in maintaining daily compliance with the department's standards of performance, and least important to audit quality control reviews, auditor position/job descriptions, and auditor performance appraisals.

Audit Manual

The need to issue formal manuals will largely depend on the size of the department. Any department with five or more staff members, or whose auditors work alone, should probably have one. The manual should address such things as administrative matters (e.g., progress reports, time and attendance, travel), adherence to the department's guidelines, relationships with auditees, auditing techniques, reporting audit results, and working paper standards (whether paper media, electronic media, or a combination).

Staff Meetings

- Staff meetings are conducted periodically to improve communications.

- Audit staff are afforded a venue where problems are discussed and receive updates regarding departmental policies.

- The CAE can address rumors affecting the audit department and the company.

Audit Reports

A report issued by an internal auditor should contain an expression of opinion when an opinion will improve communications with the reader of the report. Due professional care requires that the auditor's opinions be based on sufficient factual evidence that warrants the expression of the opinions. Due care does not require the performance of extensive audit examination. It calls for reasonable work.

The type of audit report (final, interim, or combination), the form of communication (oral, written, or combination), the type of audience to receive the audit report (internal management, external auditors, or combination), and the type of participants (by job title in the audit and the auditee department) to attend the entrance conference and the exit audit conference should be spelled out in the audit department policies and procedures manual.

An audit policy should require that final audit reports not be issued without a management response. However, when an audit with significant findings is complete except for management's response, the best alternative is to issue an *interim* report regarding the important issues noted. This is because time is of the essence here.

The final audit report should be reviewed, approved, and signed by the director of internal auditing or his designee. When illegal acts are being performed by several of the highest-ranking officers of the company, the audit report should be addressed to the audit committee of the board of directors.

Follow-Up

The CAE should ensure follow-up of prior audit findings and recommendations to determine whether corrective action was taken and is achieving the desired results. If the auditor finds that no corrective action has been taken on a prior audit finding that is still valid, the auditor should determine whether management or the board has assumed the risk of not taking corrective action.

Personnel Management and Development

The CAE should establish a program for selecting and developing the human resources of the internal auditing department. A well-developed set of selection criteria is a key factor in the success of an audit department's human resource program.

Hiring

The audit staff should include members proficient in applying internal auditing standards, procedures, and techniques. When hiring an entry-level audit staff, the most likely predictors of an applicant's success as an auditor would be the ability to organize and express thoughts well; the least likely predictors would be: grade point average on college accounting courses; ability to fit well socially into a group; and the level of detail of knowledge of the company. When hiring an auditor, reasonable assurance should be obtained as to each prospective auditor's qualifications and proficiency. It should include obtaining college transcript(s), checking an applicant's references, and determining previous job experience.

Selection Criteria

The CAE should establish the evaluation criteria for the selection of new internal audit staff members. Criteria would be an appreciation of the fundamentals of accounting, an understanding of management principles, and the ability to recognize deviations from good business practices. Criteria would not include proficiency in computerized operations and the use of computers in auditing.

Performance Criteria

The CAE should establish guidelines for evaluating the performance of audit staff members: the evaluator should justify very high and very low evaluations because of their impact on the employee; evaluations should be made annually or more frequently to provide the employee with feedback about competence; and the first evaluation should be made shortly after commencing work to serve as an early guide to the new employee. But the evaluator should not use standard evaluation comments, because there are so many employees whose performance is completely satisfactory. The performance appraisal system for evaluating an auditor should include specific accomplishments directly related to the performance of the audit program.

Continuing Education

The CAE is responsible for establishing continuing education and training opportunities to develop the human resources of the audit department. The main purpose of audit department training is to achieve both individual and departmental goals in training.

External Auditors

The CAE should coordinate internal and external audit efforts to minimize duplication of audit work and to increase the effectiveness of audit work.

Quality Assurance

The CAE should establish and maintain a quality assurance program to evaluate the operations of the internal auditing department. The standard calls for three elements for the quality assurance program: supervision, internal reviews, and external reviews. The audit department should have periodic quality assurance reviews. Accomplishing the intended results and demonstrating consistent quality are also part of the quality assurance task.

Postaudit Quality Review

The postaudit quality review provides top managers with an independent assessment of the extent to which the audit organization complies with professional standards and its own policies and procedures.

Reviewing individual assignments provides valuable feedback to managers on how well-selected auditable units consistently achieve the expected quality. The number and type of assignments selected for testing should provide a reasonable basis for making this assessment.

Assurance Audit Engagements

Assurance auditing provides an assessment of the reliability and/or relevance of data and operations in specific areas of business functions. The scope of work includes third-party and contract audit, quality audit, due diligence audit, security audit, privacy audit, performance audit, operational audit, financial audit, IT audit, and compliance audit. With these engagements, internal auditors provide reasonable assurance whether organizational goals are being accomplished.

Audits of Third Parties

There will be at least three parties to several business transactions such as electronic procurement, electronic payment, computer-based applications service providers (ASPs), computer system outsourcing services, and computer service bureaus. Key parties include the purchaser, the third-party provider, and the supplier. The purpose of third-party auditing is to ensure that controls are adequate and that proper evidence is collected in the event of a dispute between the parties.

The internal auditor should review general controls and transaction controls at the third-party provider's computer center. Examples of general controls include system development and program change controls; security and access control methods; backup, recovery, and business continuity controls; operating system controls; and audit trails. Examples of transaction controls include transaction authorization, accuracy, completeness, compensating, and user controls.

Audit of Contracts

Many opportunities exist in contract auditing in terms of cost recovery in such areas as fraud, kickbacks, overcharges, and conflict of interest. Similar to IT system development audits, internal auditors should participate early in contract audits such as construction audits. Early participation is required in bidding procedures, cost estimates, contractual terms, contractors' accounting (billing) systems, cost control, and project control procedures. A provision should be provided in the contract for overall project reviews, billing reviews, progress reviews, and cost recovery audits.

Quality Audit Engagements

Quality Audit of a Company's Products or Services

Most organizations view quality of a product or service as a competitive weapon. Quality can increase revenues and sales, decrease costs, and increase profits. The internal audit scope of quality function includes review of the charter, organization chart, quality policies and procedures, quality control tools, quality costs (cost of quality), quality management tools, quality standards, applicable laws and regulations, and Six Sigma metrics.

Quality Audit of Internal Audit Function

Many audit departments have installed total quality management (TQM) approaches to improve audit operations. There are eight steps to TQM in audit operations:

1. Initial quality assessment

2. Chief audit executive awareness

3. Formation of a quality council

4. Fostering teamwork in audits

5. Development of prototypes

6. Celebration of success

7. Organizational implementation

8. Annual audit quality review

Due Diligence Audit Engagements

Due diligence audits are team-based effort with internal auditors, external auditors, lawyers, engineers, IT staff, and other specialists. Three phases in this audit include information gathering (phase 1), information analysis (phase 2), and information reporting (phase 3). Information gathering involves collecting information through document reviews, interviews, and meetings. Information analysis may include analytical reviews, including ratio analysis, regression analysis, and other quantitative techniques. Information reporting includes writing a balanced report based on facts with an executive summary. In addition to writing reports, oral reports can be used for immediate response and clarification of issues and findings.

Security Audit Engagements

The scope of security audits, which can be unannounced audits, includes logical security, physical security, computer storage medium, and safety. Logical security focuses on determining whether a person attempting access should be allowed into a computer system and what the user can do once on the system. Specific controls in logical review include authentication controls such as composition and change of passwords and user identification codes (IDs), encryption methods and routines, and restricting transactions to particular terminals and employees. Terminal-related controls include time-out limits and displaying the last time and date a user ID was used.

Privacy Audit Engagements

Privacy is the right of an individual to limit access to information regarding that individual. The term "privacy" refers to the social balance between an individual's right to keep information confidential and the societal benefit derived from sharing information, and how this balance is codified to give individuals the means to control personal information. The term "confidentiality" refers to disclosure of information only to authorized individuals and entities.

The organization can protect itself from privacy and confidentiality problems by developing a policy statement and by showing the amount of damage done by the accused.

In general, internal auditors are concerned about accidental or intentional disclosure of confidential data. They are also concerned about collection and use of such data. Legal requirements dictate the collection, disclosure, and use of data, both in public and private sectors. Internal auditors must understand that there is a trade-off between the level of protection (security) and the cost of that protection and that there is no absolute (perfect) security.

Performance Audit Engagements

Any operation or function, whether it is production or service, needs to be measured in terms of its performance. To measure performance, performance standards, which are tied to the primary objectives of the operation or function, must be developed and monitored. In addition, each performance standard must be expressed in terms of efficiency and effectiveness criteria. If too many performance standards or indicators exist, employees may not be able to handle them properly, which can lead to a waste of resources. Therefore, both management and employees should focus on a few meaningful key performance indicators (KPIs).

Operational Audit Engagements

The economic events and business transactions of an entity are usually classified into several cycles for convenience of grouping similar and related activities, and in order to manage the audit effectively and efficiently. For example, typical cycles for a manufacturing organization include:

- Revenue

- Expenditure

- Production/conversion

- Treasury (financing/investing)

- Financial reporting (external)

The production/conversion cycle is the only one that will be different between manufacturing and nonmanufacturing organizations. Regardless of the nature of the organization, an internal control structure must meet several detailed internal control objectives to prevent, detect, and correct errors, omissions, fraud, and irregularities during handling of the business transaction cycles.

Introduction to Revenue Cycle

Major audit activities in a revenue cycle would include:

Revenue — Credit Management

- List all shipments exceeding the customer credit limits in order to understand reasons of noncompliance.

- Compare the percentage of credit applications that were rejected with standards to determine whether the credit approval process is strict or lax.

Revenue — Billing

- Compare shipping records with sales invoices by line item for testing to determine whether all inventory shipments were billed to customers.

- Identify discrepancies between quantities shipped and quantities billed for understanding reasons.

- Use "controlled reprocessing" techniques to identify lost or incomplete sales accounting record updates.

Introduction to Revenue Cycle (continued)

Revenue — Accounts Receivable

- Develop a control total to verify that the dollar amounts for all debits and credits for incoming transactions are posted properly and completely to an accounts receivable master file.

- Recompute provisions for doubtful accounts and compare with management's estimates.

- List all credit balances for further analysis and interpretation because debit balances are normal.

- List all outstanding receivables balances in excess of customer credit limits for understanding reasons of noncompliance.

- Recompute customer receivables account-aging categories, and compare them with management's computations.

Revenue — Cash Receipts

- List outstanding customer payment checks that were not applied to their account receivables records.

- Compare the accuracy of posting of cash receipts journal entries to general ledger cash accounts.

Introduction to Revenue Cycle (continued)

Revenue — Commissions

- Recompute sales commissions to salespersons and distributors, and compare them with management calculations and contracts.

- Verify that sales commissions were adjusted to reflect customer returns and other credits not resulting in a sale.

Introduction to Expenditure Cycle

Major audit activities in an expenditure cycle would include:

Purchasing

- Produce a list of all purchase transactions processed after the cut-off date in order to determine whether all material liabilities for trade accounts payable have been recorded.

- List all new suppliers/vendors to determine whether they were properly approved with competitive bids obtained, where applicable.

- List all suppliers or vendors who exceeded certain dollar threshold limits (e.g., budgets) for further analysis and justification of doing business with them.

- List the top 10 suppliers or vendors for further analysis and identification of improprieties or irregularities, if any.

Accounts Payable

- Identify unauthorized vendors in a vendor database for testing to determine existence of valid recorded liabilities. The presence of unauthorized vendors is an indication of fraud and overstates liabilities.

Introduction to Expenditure Cycle (continued)

- Identify debit balances for further analysis and interpretation since credit balances are normal.

- Use the test data method to test the accuracy of application program controls over the purchase transactions.

- List payable balances with no scheduled payment date, which is an indication of a lapse in procedures.

- Recompute the file balance to reconcile the accounts payable balance listed in the company's month-end trial balance report to the master accounts payable file.

- Use generalized audit software to verify that all purchases were authorized, that all goods paid for were received, and that there were no duplicate payments.

Personnel Administration

- List employees who have not taken vacations, which is an indication of a fraud.

- List employees who have taken excessive sick leave, which is an indication of an abuse.

- Compare employee pay rates used in calculating payroll to official pay rates to find out discrepancies.

Introduction to Expenditure Cycle (continued)

Payroll

- Use the test data method to test the accuracy of computations of employee withholding for tax and benefit deductions, and compare the actual results with predetermined results. Identify unusually small tax deductions.

- Use the parallel simulation technique to ensure that the payroll program is reliable and to test the accuracy of the payroll calculation.

- Use the test data method to test calculation of regular and overtime pay amounts and compare the results with predetermined or expected results.

- Produce a cross-reference list after matching individual employee payroll time card information to personnel department records and files to conclude that individuals are bona fide employees.

- Compare current period amounts with previous period amounts for employee gross and net payroll wages. Identify employees with unusual pay amounts after performing reasonableness tests.

- Select all transactions in specified activity codes and in excess of predetermined amounts. Trace them to proper authorization in personnel files in order to determine if payroll changes are authorized.

Introduction to Production/Conversion Cycle

Major audit activities in a production/conversion cycle would include:

Inventory Control

- Use "tagging and tracing" techniques to provide a computer trail of all relevant processing steps applied to a specific inventory transaction in an online perpetual inventory system. To accomplish this, certain file-updating transactions need to be selected for detailed testing. Inquiry-type transactions will not be useful since they are merely data lookups, with no file updating. File updating is a critical, risky activity since the file contents can be changed.

- List old or slow-moving inventory items for possible write-offs.

- List large differences between the last physical inventory and the perpetual book inventory for further analysis and review of adjustments.

- Test the numerical sequence of physical inventory count sheet numbers to account for all numbers, whether used or not.

- List inventory items with negative balances for further analysis and follow-up.

- Test the accuracy of reduction of inventory relief for cost of sales.

Introduction to Production/Conversion Cycle (continued)

- Calculate inventory turnovers by product (including finished goods, raw materials, and WIP components), and compare them to targets.

- Use the control flowcharting technique to review the overall business control context of the work-in-process computer processing application system. This technique is similar to a normal flowchart except that it will focus more on controls and control points in a work-in-process flow in a manufacturing environment.

Production Control

- List production orders with no due date of production scheduling and no delivery (shipping) date.

- Compare production counts between production system records and cost accounting system records to ensure that costs are allocated based on correct production count.

- Test the accuracy of accumulation of production costs.

Introduction to Production/Conversion Cycle (continued)

Shipping

- List customer orders that were shipped late by comparing order due date on production records with shipped date on shipping records.

- Identify items shipped but not billed, which is an indication of lapse in procedures.

Traffic

- Compare the billed rates to the contract rates and analyze the rate differences.

- Compare the actual claims filed for loss or damage this year to previous years and analyze the trends in claims.

Quality Control

- Compare the number of nonconforming materials used in production this year to previous years and analyze the reasons for the differences.

- Compare the actual number of sample inspections performed this year to a current target or previous year's actual and target and analyze the reasons for the differences.

Introduction to Production/Conversion Cycle (continued)

Fixed Assets

- List high-dollar-value assets for physical inspection.

- List asset additions and disposal for vouching to supporting documentation.

- List high-dollar-value maintenance expenses for possible capitalization.

- List fully depreciated assets.

- Compare depreciation periods with guidelines provided by management and tax authorities for compliance, and list unusually long or short depreciation periods.

- List assets without any depreciation charges, which would increase income.

- Use the parallel simulation audit technique to calculate depreciation charges using the declining balance method.

Introduction to Production/Conversion Cycle (continued)

Plant Maintenance

- Compare the maintenance budget this year to previous years and analyze the reasons for the increase or decrease.

- Compare the actual labor and material costs incurred this year to previous years and analyze the reasons for the increase or decrease.

Cost Accounting

- Use the test data method to determine whether all overhead is completely allocated to cost centers by the computer program.

- List large cost variances (between standard and actual) for further analysis and interpretations.

- Recompute inventory valuation and compare it with actual.

- Compare cost of sales data between summary totals and aggregation of individual item totals to ensure that they are the same.

- Test the accuracy of the accumulation of production costs by cross-referencing to the production system.

Introduction to Production/Conversion Cycle (continued)

Variance Calculations

Ensure that the **burden expenditure variance** is calculated as:

Actual indirect manufacturing expense incurred − Allowed burden at actual activity level (fixed plus variable) = Burden expenditure variance

Ensure that the **burden efficiency variance** is calculated as:

Actual direct labor hours at the fixed portions of the burden rate − Standard direct labor hours earned at the fixed portion of the burden rate = Burden efficiency variance

Ensure that the **burden volume variance** is calculated as:

Actual direct labor hours at the fixed portions of the burden rate − Budgeted direct labor hours at the fixed portion of the burden rate = Burden volume variance

Basic Definitions of Variances

Lot size variance. It is the difference between the standard number of units in a standard lot size and the actual number of units in actual lot size times the standard unit setup cost.

Introduction to Production/Conversion Cycle (continued)

Rework variance. It is calculated as the cost of actual labor hours at the standard rate plus the standard labor burden plus any material required at the standard cost to correct defective production to meet engineering specifications.

Scrap variance. It is calculated as the difference between the actual weight of recovered residual material and the standard allowed weight times the standard scrap price.

Spoilage variance. It is calculated as the full standard cost through the last completed operation of spoiled production that does not meet specifications and cannot be reworked to meet specifications less the standard cost of any salvaged parts or components.

Standard revision variance. It is calculated as the difference between the old standard and a new standard cost in those cases when standards are revised in the period between general revisions for operating measurements, but the standard cost documents and inventory pricing are left unchanged until the next general revision.

Introduction to Treasury Cycle

Major audit activities in a treasury cycle would include:

Debt Management

- List securities for physical inspection or confirmation.

- List interest payments for vouching to supporting documentation.

- List unusual interest rates on loans after comparing them with management guidelines; unusual rates could indicate a fraudulent situation.

- Conduct reasonableness test between interest amount paid and principal amount for each category of debt and for aggregate.

Equity Management

- List capital stock purchases, sales, and redemptions for vouching with supporting documentation.

- Recompute profits and losses on redemption of stock for accuracy and completeness.

Introduction to Treasury Cycle (continued)

Investment Management

- Recalculate amortization of discounts and premiums on investment accounts, and compare them with management calculations.

- Compare interest and dividend records with investment registers for determining relationships between accounts. Conduct reasonableness tests between the interest amount and the principal amounts of the investment.

- Recompute profits and losses on disposal of investments for accuracy and completeness.

Dividends Management

- List dividend payments for vouching with supporting documentation.

- List unusual dividend rates applied to capital stock.

- List missing check numbers for making dividend payments for further analysis.

Introduction to Treasury Cycle (continued)

- Compare dividend records with stock registers to prove that dividends are for the valid stocks.

- Conduct reasonableness test between total dividend amounts paid and the average number of shares and dollar aggregate.

Introduction to Financial Reporting Cycle

Major audit activities in a financial reporting cycle would include:

Tax Accounting and Reporting

- In order to detect whether sales taxes are applied properly and computed correctly, sort sales orders by geographic area, compute taxes in aggregate, and compare the aggregate amount with the sum of individual taxes charged for each geographic area.

- Perform reasonableness tests between taxes actually collected and the taxes that should have been collected. Identify discrepancies.

Financial Audit Engagements

Financial auditing is defined as determining whether financial statements present fairly the financial position and results of operations. More specifically, financial auditing provides reasonable assurance about whether the financial statements of an audited entity present fairly the financial position, results of operations, and cash flows in accordance with generally accepted accounting principles (GAAP). Balance sheet and income statements are the focus; balance sheets provide the financial status of an entity at the end of an accounting period, while income statements report income earned during an accounting period.

The **purpose and scope of a financial audit** are to determine whether the overall financial statements of an entity are prepared and reported in accordance with specified criteria (standards). The audit scope is usually limited to accounting-related data. Financial audits are conducted by independent auditors who are "external" to the organization being audited. External auditors express an opinion on the overall fairness of the financial statements. The audit report contains the auditor's opinion. Four types of audit opinions can be included in an audit report:

1. Unqualified opinion

2. Qualified opinion

3. Adverse opinion

4. Disclaimer opinion

Financial Audit Engagements (continued)

However, only one type of opinion can be included in any one report.

A suggested framework for describing the general audit and control procedures performed by external auditors for conducting **financial audits** is:

- Obtain background information about the client.

- Assess preliminary risks and exposures.

- Obtain an understanding of the client's internal control structure.

- Develop an audit plan and audit program.

- Perform compliance tests of controls.

- Perform substantive tests of transactions and account balances.

- Evaluate test results.

- Form an audit opinion.

- Issue the audit report.

Financial Audit Engagements (continued)

General audit objectives for a **financial review** are:

- To evaluate whether the account balances appear reasonable in the financial statements

- To determine whether the amounts included in the financial statements are valid

- To determine whether all amounts that should be included have actually been included in the financial statements

- To ensure that assets included in the financial statements are owned by the entity and liabilities belong to the entity

- To determine whether the amounts included in the financial statements are properly valued

- To determine whether correct amounts are included in the correct accounts and those accounts are properly classified in financial statements

- To determine whether transactions near the balance sheet date are recorded in the proper accounting period

Financial Audit Engagements (continued)

- To determine whether details in the account balance agree with related subsidiary ledger amounts, foot to the total in the account balance, and agree with the total in the general ledger

- To ensure that all balance sheet and income statements accounts and related information are correctly disclosed in the financial statements and properly described in the body and footnotes of the statements

Information Technology Audit Engagements

Information Systems Audit Scope

Information system audits deal with the review of computer operations and application systems where computer equipment is located and computer-based systems are used. The purpose and scope of information systems audits are to determine whether controls over computer systems and information technology assets are adequate. These particular types of audits are conducted by Information Systems (IS) auditors, who may be external or internal to the organization being audited.

Materiality, as it relates to information technology (IT) audits, considers the issues for both financial and operational audit situations. Specifically, it deals with issues such as the impact of computer operations control weaknesses on the organization's financial and operating records; impact of system integrity and security control weaknesses on the application system's data and system usefulness to users; and impact of system errors and irregularities on the financial statements.

Information Systems Control Objectives

An internal control structure must meet several detailed information systems control objectives to prevent, detect, and correct errors, omissions, irregularities, and computer intrusions, (such as viruses and worms), and to recover from such activities to ensure continuity of business operations. Here the term "system" includes hardware, data, software, people, documentation, and the associated procedures, whether manual or automated.

Information systems control objectives are:

- System assets are safeguarded.

- System reliability is ensured.

- Data integrity is maintained.

- System security is ensured.

- System availability is ensured.

- System controllability is maintained.

Information Systems Control Objectives (continued)

- System maintainability is ensured.

- System usability is ensured.

- System effectiveness is ensured.

- System economy and efficiency are maintained.

- System quality is maintained.

Information Systems Audit Objectives

- Ensure that adequate audit coverage of major risks and exposures in an IS environment is available.

- Ensure that IT resources are allocated to computer hardware, peripheral equipment, software, services, and personnel in an efficient and effective manner to achieve the IT department and the organization's goals and objectives.

- Provide reasonable assurance that computer-related assets (e.g., data, programs, facilities, equipment, and supplies) are safeguarded.

- Ensure that information is timely, accurate, available, and reliable.

- Provide reasonable assurance that all errors, omissions, and irregularities are prevented, detected, corrected, and reported.

- Obtain the most efficient usage of audit resources (staff time and money).

Information Systems Audit and Control Procedures

- Obtain background information about the IT operations and the systems.

- Conduct a preliminary evaluation of internal controls.

- Develop an audit plan and audit program.

- Perform compliance tests of controls.

- Perform substantive tests of transactions and account balances.

- Evaluate the test results and issue an audit report.

Information Systems Control Types

According to the Committee of Sponsoring Organizations (COSO) of the Treadway Commission study, with widespread reliance on information systems, controls are needed over all information systems, whether financial, operational, large, or small. Two broad groupings of information systems controls can be used. The first is **general or information technology controls**, which ensure the continued, proper operation of computer information systems. General controls are designed to focus on information systems or information technology as a whole.

The second category is **application controls**, which include computerized steps within the application software and related manual procedures to control the processing of various types of transactions. Together these controls serve to ensure completeness, accuracy, and validity of the financial and other information in the system.

Classification of Computer Controls

Computer controls can be classified in different ways. Two basic categories are (1) general controls, and (2) application controls. Another way to classify controls is by their nature, such as management controls (e.g., policies, procedures, standards, separation of duties), physical controls (e.g., access to computer facilities and equipment), and technical controls (e.g., logical access controls to programs and data files, use of options and parameters). Another way is to classify controls by functional areas, such as application controls, network controls, development controls, operations controls, security controls, and user controls. Still another way is to classify controls on the basis of action or objective, such as directive, preventive, detective, corrective, and recovery.

Cost-Benefit Analysis of Controls

A cost-benefit analysis is advised during the process of designing each type of control into an application system during its development and maintenance as well as during its operation. Ideally, costs should never exceed benefits to be derived from installing controls. However, costs should not always be the sole determining factor because it may be difficult or impractical to quantify benefits such as timeliness, improved quality and relevance of data and information, or improved customer service and system response time.

Costs versus Controls versus Convenience

Costs of controls vary with their implementation time and the complexity of the system or operation. Control implementation time is important to realize benefits from installing appropriate controls. For example, it costs significantly more to correct a design problem in the implementation phase of an application system under development than it does to address in the early planning and design phases.

Compensating Controls

Normally, auditors will find more control-related problems in first-time audits of an area. Generally, the more frequently an area is audited, the less probability of many control weaknesses. Therefore, determining the nature of efficient and effective operations needs both audit instinct and business judgment. During the control evaluation process, the auditor should consider the availability of compensating controls as a way to mitigate or minimize the impact of inadequate or incomplete controls. In essence, the concept of compensating controls deals with balancing of weak internal controls in one area with strong internal controls in other areas of the organization. Here the word "area" can include a section within a user or IT department.

Review of Compensating Controls

One way to strengthen internal controls and reduce the possibility of errors, omissions, and irregularities is to build compensating controls into operations and systems and to review their adequacy. Control-related information should be produced for review by supervisors or managers so that any irregularities are noticed for further action. Some tools and techniques that facilitate a review of compensating controls include:

- Audit trails

- Control total verifications

- Transaction logs

- Error logs

- Control grids/matrices

- Internal control questionnaires

- Bank reconciliations

Review of Compensating Controls (continued)

- Independent reviews

- Logical access security controls

- Exception and statistical reports

- Manual/automated reconciliations

- Report balancing

Interrelationships between Controls

Controls are interrelated. Lack of controls in one area may affect other interrelated areas. Similarly, what is an accepted control in one area may not be applicable to another area. This is because life cycles of a system or data are different. Different controls are required in each of the phases of a system or data life cycle.

Use of Controls

Implementation of controls requires money and other resources. Judicious use of controls is needed. Proper use of controls depends on many factors, situations, and environments. Some major common considerations are:

- Size of the IT department

- Size of the organization in which the IT department is a part

- Availability of financial and other resources

- Value of the assets and resources to be protected

- Level and complexity of computer technology in use

- Type of industry to which the organization belongs

- Risk levels of the system or operation

- Management's tolerance to risk levels

- Management's commitment to and support of controls

- Competitive position of the organization in the industry in which it operates

- Government, tax, accounting, legal, and regulatory requirements placed on the organization

Information Systems Audit Evidence

The scope includes understanding the audit evidence types and knowing the sources for gathering audit evidence.

Audit Evidence Types

The evidence produced by automated information systems, whether financial or operational, may be different from that produced by manual systems. It is important for the auditor to understand these new forms of evidence because the methods used for auditing will change as the forms of evidence change.

These new forms of evidence include transaction initiation, hard-copy input, transaction authorization, movement of documents, hard-copy processing, simplified processing, location of information, hard-copy output, file of documents, hard-copy audit trail, procedure manual, activity monitoring, segregation of duties, and bulk processing techniques.

Information Systems Audit Evidence-Gathering Sources

The information systems auditor uses one or more sources or techniques to gather audit evidence during an audit (whether it is financial or operational in nature):

- Reviewing IT organizational structure

- Reviewing IT documentation standards and practices

- Reviewing systems documentation, such as flowcharts, manuals, system/program specifications

- Interviewing appropriate personnel in both IT and functional departments

- Observing operations and employee performance of duties in both IT and functional user departments

- Using audit documentation techniques, such as flowcharts, questionnaires, system narratives, decision trees and tables, control grid charts, security clearance matrices

- Selecting and testing key controls in either the IT or the functional user department

- Applying sampling techniques, where applicable, to select sample accounts (say for confirming accounts receivable balances with customers)

Information Systems Audit Evidence-Gathering Sources (continued)

- Using computer-assisted audit techniques (CAATs) to sort, extract, compare, analyze, compute, reperform, and report the required data residing on computer data files. This can be done with the use of generalized data-extraction program report writers, third-generation programming languages (e.g., COBOL), fourth-generation programming language-based software products, fifth generation programming language, or computer audit software products.

Specific IT Audits

The scope of specific IT audit engagements can include a review of:

- Operating system audit

  - Systems software administration

  - Operating systems software

  - Systems software changes

- Application development

  - Auditor participation

  - Audit approaches

  - Auditor's role

  - Audit scope (usability, maintainability, auditability, controllability, and securability)

- Data and network communications and connections

  - Local-area networks

Specific IT Audits (continued)

- Value-added networks

- Wide-area networks

- Network changes

- Voice communications

- Systems security

  - Access control security software

  - Data security controls

  - Firewalls

  - Physical access security and environmental controls

- Contingency planning

- Databases

  - Database management systems software

Specific IT Audits (continued)

- Data dictionary systems software
- Data warehouse, data mart, and data mining
- Functional areas of IT operations
  - General operating practices
  - Data entry function
  - Report balancing and reconciliation procedures
  - Report handling and distribution procedures
  - Output error handling procedures
  - Report retention and security measures
  - Controls over microfiche and microfilm records
  - Job scheduling
  - Production job turnover

Specific IT Audits (continued)

- Computer operations

- Tape and disk management systems

- System logs

- Help-desk function

- Web infrastructure

- Software licensing

- Electronic funds transfer/electronic data interchange

  - Automated teller machine systems

  - Automated clearing house systems

  - Wire transfer systems

  - Electronic data interchange systems

- Electronic commerce and mobile commerce

Specific IT Audits (continued)

- Information protection

    - Computer viruses

    - Electronic mail

- Encryption

- Enterprise-wide resource planning software

- Operational application systems

Compliance Audit Engagements

General Audits of Compliance

- Planning, which requires an understanding of relevant laws and regulations; and testing compliance with laws and regulations

- Risk assessment, which includes vulnerability assessment (i.e., inherent risk $\times$ internal controls)

- Testing, which tests internal controls with a small sample of transactions

Specific Audits of Compliance

The scope includes environmental audits and human resource policy audits.

Environmental Audits

An environmental management system is an organization's structure of responsibilities and policies, practices, procedures, processes, and resources for protecting the environment and managing environmental issues.

The seven environmental audit categories include:

1. Compliance audits

2. Environmental management system audits

3. Transactional audits (acquisition and divestiture)

4. Treatment, storage, and disposal facility audits

5. Pollution prevention audits

6. Environmental liability accrual audits

7. Product audits (appraisal of production processes)

Human Resource Policy Audits

The scope of review for human resource policy compliance audits include:

- Safety

- Hazard communication

- Security over organization's assets

- Benefits continuation

- Bulletin boards

- Exit interview

- I-9 employment eligibility

- Independent contractors

- Telephone usage

Human Resource Policy Audits (continued)

- Smoking policy

- Drug testing

- Substance abuse policy

- Accommodating disabilities

- Sexual harassment

Consulting Engagements

Consulting engagements solve problems and make recommendations to improve a client's operations and processes by making changes. The engagement steps consist of:

- Defining problems

- Developing alternatives

- Selecting the best alternative

- Implementing the best alternative

  The scope of consulting engagements can include:

- Internal control training

- Business process review, which includes business process reengineering (BPR) and business process improvement (BPI)

Consulting Engagements (continued)

- Benchmarking, which may include internal benchmarking, competitive benchmarking, industry benchmarking, best-in-class benchmarking, process benchmarking, and strategic benchmarking

- IT system development

- Design of performance measurement systems

IIA *STANDARDS* APPLICABLE TO OPERATIONAL ROLE OF INTERNAL AUDIT

Control

The internal audit activity must assist the organization in maintaining effective controls by evaluating their effectiveness and efficiency and by promoting continuous improvement (IIA Standard 2130).

The internal audit activity must evaluate the adequacy and effectiveness of controls in responding to risks within the organization's governance, operations, and IS regarding the:

- Reliability and integrity of financial and operational information.

- Effectiveness and efficiency of operations and programs.

- Safeguarding of assets.

- Compliance with laws, regulations, policies, procedures, and contracts.

Internal auditors must incorporate knowledge of controls gained from consulting engagements into evaluation of the organization's control processes.

Assessing the Adequacy of Control Processes

1. An organization establishes and maintains effective risk management and control processes. The purpose of control processes is to support the organization in the management of risks and the achievement of its established and communicated objectives. The control processes are expected to ensure, among other things, that:

- Financial and operational information is reliable and possesses integrity.

- Operations are performed efficiently and achieve established objectives.

- Assets are safeguarded.

- Actions and decisions of the organization are in compliance with laws, regulations, and contracts.

2. Senior management's role is to oversee the establishment, administration, and assessment of the system of risk management and control processes. Among the responsibilities of the organization's line managers is the assessment of the control processes in their respective areas. Internal auditors provide varying degrees of assurance about the effectiveness of the risk management and control processes in select activities and functions of the organization.

Assessing the Adequacy of Control Processes (continued)

3. The CAE forms an overall opinion about the adequacy and effectiveness of the control processes. The expression of such an opinion by the CAE will be based on sufficient audit evidence obtained through the completion of audits and, where appropriate, reliance on the work of other assurance providers. The CAE communicates the opinion to senior management and the board.

4. The CAE develops a proposed internal audit plan to obtain sufficient evidence to evaluate the effectiveness of the control processes. The plan includes audit engagements and/or other procedures to obtain sufficient, appropriate audit evidence about all major operating units and business functions to be assessed, as well as a review of the major control processes operating across the organization. The plan should be flexible so that adjustments may be made during the year as a result of changes in management strategies, external conditions, major risk areas, or revised expectations about achieving the organization's objectives.

5. The audit plan gives special consideration to those operations most affected by recent or unexpected changes. Changes in circumstances can result, for example, from marketplace or investment conditions, acquisitions and divestitures, organizational restructuring, new systems, and new ventures.

6. In determining the expected audit coverage for the proposed audit plan, the CAE considers relevant work performed by others who provide assurances to senior management (e.g., reliance by the CAE on the work of corporate compliance officers). The CAE's audit plan also considers audit work completed by

Assessing the Adequacy of Control Processes (continued)

the external auditor and management's own assessments of its risk management process, controls, and quality improvement processes.

7. The CAE should evaluate the breadth of coverage of the proposed audit plan to determine whether the scope is sufficient to enable the expression of an opinion about the organization's risk management and control processes. The CAE should inform senior management and the board of any gaps in audit coverage that would prevent the expression of an opinion on all aspects of these processes.

8. A key challenge for the internal audit activity is to evaluate the effectiveness of the organization's control processes based on the aggregation of many individual assessments. Those assessments are largely gained from internal audit engagements, reviews of management's self-assessments, and other assurance providers' work. As the engagements progress, internal auditors communicate, on a timely basis, the findings to the appropriate levels of management so prompt action can be taken to correct or mitigate the consequences of discovered control discrepancies or weaknesses.

Assessing the Adequacy of Control Processes (continued)

9. In evaluating the overall effectiveness of the organization's control processes, the CAE considers whether:

- Significant discrepancies or weaknesses were discovered.

- Corrections or improvements were made after the discoveries.

- The discoveries and their potential consequences lead to a conclusion that a pervasive condition exists resulting in an unacceptable level of risk.

10. The existence of a significant discrepancy or weakness does not necessarily lead to the judgment that it is pervasive and poses an unacceptable risk. The internal auditor considers the nature and extent of risk exposure as well as the level of potential consequences in determining whether the effectiveness of the control processes are jeopardized and unacceptable risks exist.

11. The CAE's report on the organization's control processes is normally presented **once a year** to senior management and the board. The report states the critical role played by the control processes in the achievement of the organization's objectives. The report also describes the nature and extent of the work performed by the internal audit activity and the nature and extent of reliance on other assurance providers in formulating the opinion.

Information Reliability and Integrity

1. Internal auditors determine whether senior management and the board have a clear understanding that information reliability and integrity is a management responsibility. This responsibility includes all critical information of the organization regardless of how the information is stored. Information reliability and integrity includes accuracy, completeness, and security.

2. The CAE determines whether the internal audit activity possesses, or has access to, competent audit resources to evaluate information reliability and integrity and associated risk exposures. This includes both internal and external risk exposures and exposures relating to the organization's relationships with outside entities.

3. The CAE determines whether information reliability and integrity breaches and conditions that might represent a threat to the organization will promptly be made known to senior management, the board, and the internal audit activity.

Information Reliability and Integrity (continued)

4. Internal auditors assess the effectiveness of preventive, detective, and mitigation measures against past attacks, as appropriate, and future attempts or incidents deemed likely to occur. Internal auditors determine whether the board has been appropriately informed of threats, incidents, vulnerabilities exploited, and corrective measures.

5. Internal auditors periodically assess the organization's information reliability and integrity practices and recommend, as appropriate, enhancements to, or implementation of, new controls and safeguards. Such assessments can either be conducted as separate stand-alone engagements or integrated into other audits or engagements conducted as part of the internal audit plan. The nature of the engagement will determine the most appropriate reporting process to senior management and the board.

Evaluating an Organization's Privacy Framework

1. The failure to protect personal information with appropriate controls can have significant consequences for an organization. The failure could damage the reputation of individuals and/or the organization and expose an organization to risks that include legal liability and diminished consumer and/or employee trust.

2. Privacy definitions vary widely depending on the culture, political environment, and legislative framework of the countries in which the organization operates. Risks associated with the privacy of information encompass personal privacy (physical and psychological); privacy of space (freedom from surveillance); privacy of communication (freedom from monitoring); and privacy of information (collection, use, and disclosure of personal information by others). Personal information generally refers to information associated with a specific individual or that has identifying characteristics that, when combined with other information, can then be associated with a specific individual. It can include any factual or subjective information—recorded or not—in any form of media. Personal information could include:

- Name, address, identification numbers, family relationships.

- Employee files, evaluations, comments, social status, or disciplinary actions.

- Credit records, income, financial status.

- Medical status.

Evaluating an Organization's Privacy Framework (continued)

3. Effective control over the protection of personal information is an essential component of the governance, risk management, and control processes of an organization. The board is ultimately accountable for identifying the principal risks to the organization and implementing appropriate control processes to mitigate those risks. This includes establishing the necessary privacy framework for the organization and monitoring its implementation.

4. The internal audit activity can contribute to good governance and risk management by assessing the adequacy of management's identification of risks related to its privacy objectives and the adequacy of the controls established to mitigate those risks to an acceptable level. The internal auditor is well positioned to evaluate the privacy framework in their organization and identify the significant risks as well as the appropriate recommendations for mitigation.

5. The internal audit activity identifies the types and appropriateness of information gathered by the organization that is deemed personal or private, the collection methodology used, and whether the organization's use of that information is in accordance with its intended use and applicable legislation.

6. Given the highly technical and legal nature of privacy issues, the internal audit activity needs appropriate knowledge and competence to conduct an assessment of the risks and controls of the organization's privacy framework.

Evaluating an Organization's Privacy Framework (continued)

7. In conducting such an evaluation of the management of the organization's privacy framework, the internal auditor:

- Considers the laws, regulations, and policies relating to privacy in the jurisdictions where the organization operates.

- Liaisons with in-house legal counsel to determine the exact nature of laws, regulations, and other standards and practices applicable to the organization and the country/countries in which it operates.

- Liaisons with IT specialists to determine that information security and data protection controls are in place and regularly reviewed and assessed for appropriateness.

- Considers the level or maturity of the organization's privacy practices. Depending on the level, the internal auditor may have differing roles. The auditor may facilitate the development and implementation of the privacy program, evaluate management's privacy risk assessment to determine the needs and risk exposures of the organization, or provide assurance on the effectiveness of the privacy policies, practices, and controls across the organization. If the internal auditor assumes any responsibility for developing and implementing a privacy program, his or her independence will be impaired.

QUALITY ASSURANCE AND IMPROVEMENT PROGRAM

The CAE must develop and maintain a quality assurance and improvement program (QAIP) that covers all aspects of the internal audit activity (IIA Standard 1300).

A QAIP is designed to enable an evaluation of the internal audit activity's conformance with the definition of internal auditing and the *Standards* and an evaluation of whether internal auditors apply the Code of Ethics. The program also assesses the efficiency and effectiveness of the internal audit activity and identifies opportunities for improvement.

Establishing a Quality Assurance and Improvement Program

1. The CAE is responsible for establishing an internal audit activity whose scope of work includes the activities in the *Standards* and in the definition of internal auditing. To ensure that this occurs, Standard 1300 requires that the CAE develop and maintain a QAIP.

2. The CAE is accountable for implementing processes designed to provide reasonable assurance to the various stakeholders that the internal audit activity:

- Performs in accordance with the internal audit charter, which is consistent with the definition of internal auditing, the Code of Ethics, and the *Standards*.

- Operates in an effective and efficient manner.

- Is perceived by those stakeholders as adding value and improving the organization's operations.

These processes include appropriate supervision, periodic internal assessments and ongoing monitoring of quality assurance, and periodic external assessments.

Establishing a Quality Assurance and Improvement Program (continued)

3. The QAIP needs to be sufficiently comprehensive to encompass all aspects of operation and management of an internal audit activity, as found in the definition of internal auditing, the Code of Ethics, the *Standards*, and best practices of the profession. The QAIP process is performed by or under direct supervision of the CAE. Except in small internal audit activities, the CAE would usually delegate most QAIP responsibilities to subordinates. In large or complex environments (e.g., numerous business units and/or locations), the CAE establishes a formal QAIP function—headed by an internal audit executive—independent of the audit and consulting segments of the internal audit activity. This executive (and limited staff) administers and monitors the activities needed for a successful QAIP.

Requirements of the Quality Assurance and Improvement Program

The QAIP must include both internal and external assessments (IIA Standard 1310).

1. A QAIP is an ongoing and periodic assessment of the entire spectrum of audit and consulting work performed by the internal audit activity. These ongoing and periodic assessments are composed of rigorous, comprehensive processes; continuous supervision and testing of internal audit and consulting work; and periodic validations of conformance with the definition of internal auditing, the Code of Ethics, and the *Standards*. This also includes ongoing measurements and analyses of performance metrics (e.g., internal audit plan accomplishment, cycle time, recommendations accepted, and customer satisfaction). If the assessments' results indicate areas for improvement by the internal audit activity, the CAE will implement the improvements through the QAIP.

2. Assessments evaluate and conclude on the quality of the internal audit activity and lead to recommendations for appropriate improvements. QAIPs include an evaluation of:

- Conformance with the definition of internal auditing, the Code of Ethics, and the *Standards*, including timely corrective actions to remedy any significant instances of nonconformance.

- Adequacy of the internal audit activity's charter, goals, objectives, policies, and procedures.

Focus on: **Managing the Internal Audit Function (40–50%)**   **140**

Requirements of the Quality Assurance and Improvement Program (continued)

- Contribution to the organization's governance, risk management, and control processes.

- Compliance with applicable laws, regulations, and government or industry standards.

- Effectiveness of continuous improvement activities and adoption of best practices.

- The extent to which the internal audit activity adds value and improves the organization's operations.

3. The QAIP efforts also include follow-up on recommendations involving appropriate and timely modification of resources, technology, processes, and procedures.

4. To provide accountability and transparency, the CAE communicates the results of external and, as appropriate, internal quality program assessments to the various stakeholders of the activity (such as senior management, the board, and external auditors). At least annually, the CAE reports to senior management and the board on the quality program efforts and results.

Internal Assessments

Internal assessments must include:

- Ongoing monitoring of the performance of the internal audit activity.

- Periodic reviews performed through self-assessment or by other persons within the organization with sufficient knowledge of internal audit practices (IIA Standard 1311).

Ongoing monitoring is an integral part of the day-to-day supervision, review, and measurement of the internal audit activity. Ongoing monitoring is incorporated into the routine policies and practices used to manage the internal audit activity and uses processes, tools, and information considered necessary to evaluate conformance with the definition of internal auditing, the Code of Ethics, and the *Standards*.

Periodic reviews are assessments conducted to evaluate conformance with the definition of internal auditing, the Code of Ethics, and the *Standards*.

Sufficient knowledge of internal audit practices requires at least an understanding of all elements of the International Professional Practices Framework.

Internal Assessments (continued)

1. The processes and tools used in ongoing internal assessments include:

- Engagement supervision,

- Checklists and procedures (e.g., in an audit and procedures manual) are being followed,

- Feedback from audit customers and other stakeholders,

- Selective peer reviews of working papers by staff not involved in the respective audits,

- Project budgets, timekeeping systems, audit plan completion, and cost recoveries, and/or

- Analyses of other performance metrics (such as cycle time and recommendations accepted).

2. Conclusions are developed as to the quality of ongoing performance and follow-up action taken to ensure appropriate improvements are implemented.

3. The IIA's *Quality Assessment Manual*, or a comparable set of guidance and tools, should serve as the basis for periodic internal assessments.

Internal Assessments (continued)

4. Periodic internal assessments may:

- Include more in-depth interviews and surveys of stakeholder groups.

- Be performed by members of the internal audit activity (self-assessment).

- Be performed by Certified Internal Auditors (CIAs) or other competent audit professionals, currently assigned elsewhere in the organization.

- Encompass a combination of self-assessment and preparation of materials subsequently reviewed by CIAs or other competent audit professionals.

- Include benchmarking of the internal audit activity's practices and performance metrics against relevant best practices of the internal audit profession.

Internal Assessments *(continued)*

5. A periodic internal assessment performed within a short time before an external assessment can serve to facilitate and reduce the cost of the external assessment. If the periodic internal assessment is performed by a qualified, independent external reviewer or review team, the assessment results should not communicate any assurances on the outcome of the subsequent external quality assessment. The report may offer suggestions and recommendations to enhance the practices of internal audit activities. If the external assessment takes the form of a self-assessment with independent validation, the periodic internal assessment can serve as the self-assessment portion of this process.

6. Conclusions are developed as to quality of performance and appropriate action initiated to achieve improvements and conformity to the *Standards*, as necessary.

7. The CAE establishes a structure for reporting results of internal assessments that maintains appropriate credibility and objectivity. Generally, those assigned responsibility for conducting ongoing and periodic reviews report to the CAE while performing the reviews and communicate results directly to the CAE.

8. At least annually, the CAE reports the results of internal assessments, necessary action plans, and their successful implementation to senior management and the board.

External Assessments

External assessments must be conducted at least once every **five years** by a qualified, independent reviewer or review team from outside the organization. The CAE must discuss with the board:

- The need for more frequent external assessments.

- The qualifications and independence of the external reviewer or review team, including any potential conflict of interest.

A qualified reviewer or review team demonstrates competence in two areas: the professional practice of internal auditing and the external assessment process. Competence can be demonstrated through a mixture of experience and theoretical learning. Experience gained in organizations of similar size, complexity, sector or industry, and technical issues is more valuable than less relevant experience. In the case of a review team, not all members of the team need to have all the competencies; it is the team as a whole that is qualified. The CAE uses professional judgment when assessing whether a reviewer or review team demonstrates sufficient competence to be qualified.

An "independent reviewer or review team" means not having either a real or an apparent conflict of interest and not being a part of, or under the control of, the organization to which the internal audit activity belongs (IIA Standard 1312).

External Assessments (continued)

1. External assessments cover the entire spectrum of audit and consulting work performed by the internal audit activity and should not be limited to assessing its QAIP. To achieve optimum benefits from an external assessment, the scope of work should include benchmarking, identification, and reporting of leading practices that could assist the internal audit activity in becoming more efficient and/or effective. This can be accomplished through either a full external assessment by a qualified, independent external reviewer or review team or a comprehensive internal self-assessment with independent validation by a qualified, independent external reviewer or review team. Nonetheless, the CAE is to ensure the scope clearly states the expected deliverables of the external assessment in each case.

2. External assessments of an internal audit activity contain an expressed opinion as to the entire spectrum of assurance and consulting work performed (or that should have been performed based on the internal audit charter) by the internal audit activity, including its conformance with the definition of internal auditing, the Code of Ethics, and the *Standards* and, as appropriate, includes recommendations for improvement. Apart from conformance with the definition of internal auditing, the Code of Ethics, and the *Standards*, the scope of the assessment is adjusted at the discretion of the CAE, senior management, or the board. These assessments can have considerable value to the CAE and other members of the internal audit activity, especially when benchmarking and best practices are shared.

External Assessments (continued)

3. On completion of the review, a formal communication is to be given to senior management and the board.

4. There are two approaches to external assessments. The first approach is a full external assessment conducted by a qualified, independent external reviewer or review team. This approach involves an outside team of competent professionals under the leadership of an experienced and professional project manager. The second approach involves the use of a qualified, independent external reviewer or review team to conduct an independent validation of the internal self-assessment and a report completed by the internal audit activity. Independent external reviewers should be well versed in leading internal audit practices.

5. Individuals who perform the external assessment are free from any obligation to, or interest in, the organization whose internal audit activity is the subject of the external assessment or the personnel of such organization. Particular matters relating to independence, which are to be considered by the CAE in consultation with the board, in selecting a qualified, independent external reviewer or review team include:

- Any real or apparent conflict of interest of firms that provide:

  - The external audit of financial statements.

  - Significant consulting services in the areas of governance, risk management, financial reporting, internal control, and other related areas.

External Assessments (continued)

- Assistance to the internal audit activity. The significance and amount of work performed by the professional service provider is to be considered in the deliberation.

- Any real or apparent conflict of interest of former employees of the organization who would perform the assessment. Consideration should be given to the length of time the individual has been independent of the organization.

- Individuals who perform the assessment are independent of the organization whose internal audit activity is the subject of the assessment and do not have any real or apparent conflict of interest. "Independent of the organization" means not a part of, or under the control of, the organization to which the internal audit activity belongs. In the selection of a qualified, independent external reviewer or review team, consideration is to be given to any real or apparent conflict of interest the reviewer may have due to present or past relationships with the organization or its internal audit activity, including the reviewer's participation in internal quality assessments.

- Individuals in another department of the subject organization or in a related organization, although organizationally separate from the internal audit activity, are not considered independent for purposes of conducting an external assessment. A "related organization" may be a parent organization; an affiliate in the same

External Assessments (continued)

group of entities; or an entity with regular oversight, supervision, or quality assurance responsibilities with respect to the subject organization.

- Real or apparent conflict involving peer review arrangements. Peer review arrangements between three or more organizations (e.g., within an industry or other affinity group, regional association, or other group of organizations—except as precluded by the "related organization" definition in the previous point) may be structured in a manner that alleviates independence concerns, but care is taken to ensure that the issue of independence does not arise. Peer reviews between two organizations would not pass the independence test.

- To overcome concerns of the appearance or reality of impairment of independence in instances such as those discussed in this section, one or more independent individuals could be part of the external assessment team to independently validate the work of that external assessment team.

6. Integrity requires reviewer(s) to be honest and candid within the constraints of confidentiality. Service and the public trust should not be subordinated to personal gain and advantage. Objectivity is a state of mind and a quality that lends value to a reviewer(s) services. The principle of objectivity imposes the obligation to be impartial, intellectually honest, and free of conflict of interest.

External Assessments (continued)

7. Performing and communicating the results of an external assessment require the exercise of professional judgment. Accordingly, an individual serving as an external reviewer should:

- Be a competent, CIA professional who possesses current, in-depth knowledge of the *Standards*.

- Be well versed in the best practices of the profession.

- Have at least three years of recent experience in the practice of internal auditing or related consulting at a management level.

Leaders of independent review teams and external reviewers who independently validate the results of the self-assessment should have an additional level of competence and experience gained from working previously as a team member on an external quality assessment, successful completion of the IIA's quality assessment training course or similar training, and CAE or comparable senior internal audit management experience.

8. The reviewer(s) should possess relevant technical expertise and industry experience. Individuals with expertise in other specialized areas may assist the team. For example, specialists in enterprise risk management (ERM), IT auditing, statistical sampling, operations monitoring systems, or control self-assessment may participate in certain segments of the assessment.

External Assessments (continued)

9. The CAE involves senior management and the board in determining the approach and selection of an external quality assessment provider.

10. The external assessment consists of a broad scope of coverage that includes the following elements of the internal audit activity:

- Conformance with the definition of internal auditing, the Code of Ethics, and the *Standards*; and the internal audit activity's charter, plans, policies, procedures, practices, and applicable legislative and regulatory requirements

- Expectations of the internal audit activity expressed by the board, senior management, and operational managers

- Integration of the internal audit activity into the organization's governance process, including the relationships between and among the key groups involved in the process

- Tools and techniques employed by the internal audit activity

- Mix of knowledge, experience, and disciplines within the staff, including staff focus on process improvement

External Assessments (continued)

- Determination as to whether the internal audit activity adds value and improves the organization's operations.

11. The preliminary results of the review are discussed with the CAE during and at the conclusion of the assessment process. Final results are communicated to the CAE or other official who authorized the review for the organization, preferably with copies sent directly to appropriate members of senior management and the board.

12. The communication includes:

- An opinion on the internal audit activity's conformance with the definition of internal auditing, the Code of Ethics, and the *Standards* based on a structured rating process. The term "conformance" means the practices of the internal audit activity, taken as a whole, satisfy the requirements of the definition of internal auditing, the Code of Ethics, and the *Standards*. Similarly, "nonconformance" means the impact and severity of the deficiencies in the practices of the internal audit activity are so significant they impair the internal audit activity's ability to discharge its responsibilities. The degree of "partial conformance" with the definition of internal auditing, the Code of Ethics, and/or individual *Standards*, if relevant to the overall opinion, should also be expressed in the report on the independent assessment. The expression of an opinion on

External Assessments (continued)

the results of the external assessment requires the application of sound business judgment, integrity, and due professional care.

- An assessment and evaluation of the use of best practices, both those observed during the assessment and others potentially applicable to the activity.

- Recommendations for improvement, where appropriate.

- Responses from the CAE that include an action plan and implementation dates.

13. To provide accountability and transparency, the CAE communicates the results of external quality assessments, including specifics of planned remedial actions for significant issues and subsequent information as to accomplishment of those planned actions, with the various stakeholders of the activity, such as senior management, the board, and external auditors.

External Assessments with Self-Assessment with Independent Validation

1. An external assessment by a qualified, independent reviewer or review team may be troublesome for smaller internal audit activities, or there may be circumstances in other organizations where a full external assessment by an independent team is not deemed appropriate or necessary. For example, the internal audit activity may (a) be in an industry subject to extensive regulation and/or supervision, (b) be otherwise subject to extensive external oversight and direction relating to governance and internal controls, (c) have been recently subjected to external review(s) and/or consulting services in which there was extensive benchmarking with best practices, or (d) in the judgment of the CAE, the benefits of self-assessment for staff development and the strength of the internal QAIP currently outweigh the benefits of a quality assessment by an external team.

2. A self-assessment with independent (external) validation includes:

- A comprehensive and fully documented self-assessment process, which emulates the external assessment process, at least with respect to evaluation of conformance with the definition of internal auditing, the Code of Ethics, and the *Standards*.

- An independent, on-site validation by a qualified, independent reviewer.

- Economical time and resource requirements—for example, the primary focus would be on conformance with the *Standards*.

External Assessments with Self-Assessment with Independent Validation (continued)

- Limited attention to other areas—such as benchmarking, review and consultation as to employment of leading practices, and interviews with senior and operating management—may be reduced. However, the information produced by these parts of the assessment is one of the benefits of an external assessment.

3. The same guidance and criteria as set forth in Practice Advisory 1312-1 would apply for a self-assessment with independent validation.

4. A team under the direction of the CAE performs and fully documents the self-assessment process. A draft report, similar to that for an external assessment, is prepared including the CAE's judgment on conformance with the *Standards*.

5. A qualified, independent reviewer or review team performs sufficient tests of the self-assessment so as to validate the results and express the indicated level of the activity's conformance with the definition of internal auditing, the Code of Ethics, and the *Standards*. The independent validation follows the process outlined in The IIA's *Quality Assessment Manual* or a similar comprehensive process.

External Assessments with Self-Assessment with Independent Validation (continued)

6. As part of the independent validation, the independent external reviewer —upon completion of a rigorous review of the self-assessment team's evaluation of conformance with the definition of internal auditing, the Code of Ethics, and the *Standards*:

- Reviews the draft report and attempts to reconcile unresolved issues (if any).

- If in agreement with the opinion of conformance with the definition of internal auditing, the Code of Ethics, and the *Standards*, adds wording (as needed) to the report, concurring with the self-assessment process and opinion and—to the extent deemed appropriate—in the report's findings, conclusions, and recommendations.

- If not in agreement with the evaluation, adds dissenting wording to the report, specifying the points of disagreement with it and—to the extent deemed appropriate—with the significant findings, conclusions, recommendations, and opinions in the report.

- Alternatively, may prepare a separate independent validation report— concurring or expressing disagreement as outlined above—to accompany the report of the self-assessment.

External Assessments with Self-Assessment with Independent Validation (continued)

7. The final report(s) of the self-assessment with independent validation is signed by the self-assessment team and the qualified, independent external reviewer(s) and issued by the CAE to senior management and the board.

8. To provide accountability and transparency, the CAE communicates the results of external quality assessments—including specifics of planned remedial actions for significant issues and subsequent information as to accomplishment of those planned actions—with the various stakeholders of the activity, such as senior management, the board, and external auditors.

Reporting on the Quality Assurance and Improvement Program

The CAE must communicate the results of the QAIP to senior management and the board. The form, content, and frequency of communicating the results of the QAIP is established through discussions with senior management and the board and considers the responsibilities of the internal audit activity and CAE as contained in the internal audit charter. To demonstrate conformance with the definition of internal auditing, the Code of Ethics, and the *Standards*, the results of external and periodic internal assessments are communicated upon completion of such assessments and the results of ongoing monitoring are communicated at least annually. The results include the reviewer's or review team's assessment with respect to the degree of conformance (IIA Standard 1320).

External Service Provider and Organizational Responsibility for Internal Auditing

When an external service provider serves as the internal audit activity, the provider must make the organization aware that the organization has the responsibility for maintaining an effective internal audit activity. This responsibility is demonstrated through the QAIP which assesses conformance with the definition of internal auditing, the Code of Ethics, and the *Standards* (IIA Standard 2070).

RISK-BASED INTERNAL AUDIT PLAN

Managing the Internal Audit Activity

The CAE is responsible for properly managing the internal audit activity so that:

- Audit work fulfills the general purposes and responsibilities described in the charter and approved by the board and senior management as appropriate.

- Resources of the internal audit activity are efficiently and effectively employed.

- Audit work conforms to the *International Standards for the Professional Practice of Internal Auditing (Standards)*.

Planning

The CAE should establish risk-based plans to determine the priorities of the internal audit activity, consistent with the organization's goals.

The internal audit activity's plan of engagements should be based on a risk assessment, undertaken at least annually. The input of senior management and the board should be considered in this process.

The CAE should consider accepting proposed consulting engagements based on the engagement's potential to improve management of risks, add value, and improve the organization's operations. Those engagements that have been accepted should be included in the plan.

Linking the Audit Plan to Risks and Exposures

- Any organization faces a number of uncertainties and risks that can both negatively and positively affect the organization.

- The internal audit activity's audit plan should be designed based on an assessment of risk and exposures that may affect the organization.

- The audit universe can include components from the organization's strategic plan.

- Changes in management direction, objectives, emphasis, and focus should be reflected in updates to the audit universe and related audit plan.

- Audit work schedules should be based on, among other factors, an assessment of risk priority and exposure.

- Management reporting and communication should convey risk management conclusions and recommendations to reduce exposures. For management to fully understand the degree of exposure, it is critical that audit reporting identify the criticality and consequence of the risk exposure to achieving objectives.

Communication And Approval

- The CAE should submit annually to the board for approval, and to senior management as appropriate, a summary of the internal audit activity's work schedule, staffing plan, and financial budget. The CAE should also submit all significant interim changes for approval and information. Engagement work schedules, staffing plans, and financial budgets should inform senior management and the board of the scope of internal auditing work and of any limitations placed on that scope.

- The approved engagement work schedule, staffing plan, and financial budget, along with all significant interim changes, should contain sufficient information to enable the board to ascertain whether the internal audit activity's objectives and plans support those of the organization and the board.

Resource Management

- Staffing plans and financial budgets, including the number of auditors and the knowledge, skills, and other competencies required to perform their work, should be determined from engagement work schedules, administrative activities, education and training requirements, and audit research and development efforts.

- The CAE should establish a program for selecting and developing the human resources of the internal audit activity.

- The CAE should consider using persons from co-sourcing arrangements, other consultants, or company employees from other departments to provide specialized or additional skills where needed.

Policies and Procedures

The form and content of written policies and procedures should be appropriate to the size and structure of the internal audit activity and the complexity of its work. Formal administrative and technical audit manuals may not be needed by all internal auditing entities. A small internal audit activity may be managed informally. Its audit staff may be directed and controlled through daily, close supervision and written memoranda. In a large internal audit activity, more formal and comprehensive policies and procedures are essential to guide the audit staff in the consistent compliance with the internal audit activity's standards of performance.

Coordination

- Internal and external auditing work should be coordinated to ensure adequate audit coverage and to minimize duplicate efforts.

- Oversight of the work of external auditors, including coordination with the internal audit activity, is the responsibility of the board. Actual coordination should be the responsibility of the CAE.

- In coordinating the work of internal auditors with the work of external auditors, the CAE should ensure that work to be performed by internal auditors in fulfillment of Section 2100 of the *Standards* does not duplicate the work of external auditors, which can be relied on for purposes of internal auditing coverage.

- The CAE may agree to perform work for external auditors in connection with their annual audit of the financial statements. Work performed by internal auditors to assist external auditors in fulfilling their responsibility is subject to all relevant provisions of the *Standards*.

- The CAE should make regular evaluations of the coordination between internal and external auditors.

- In exercising its oversight role, the board may request the CAE to assess the performance of external auditors.

Audit Coverage

Planned audit activities of internal and external auditors should be discussed to ensure that audit coverage is coordinated and duplicate efforts are minimized. Sufficient meetings should be scheduled during the audit process to ensure coordination of audit work and efficient and timely completion of audit activities and to determine whether observations and recommendations from work performed to date require that the scope of planned work be adjusted.

Access to Each Other's Audit Programs and Working Papers

Access to the external auditors' programs and working papers may be important in order for internal auditors to be satisfied as to the acceptability for internal audit purposes of relying on the external auditors' work. Such access carries with it the responsibility for internal auditors to respect the confidentiality of those programs and working papers. Similarly, access to the internal auditors' programs and working papers should be given to external auditors in order for external auditors to be satisfied as to the acceptability, for external audit purposes, of relying on the internal auditors' work.

Exchange of Audit Reports and Management Letters

Internal audit final communications, management's responses to those communications, and subsequent internal audit activity follow-up reviews should be made available to external auditors. These communications assist external auditors in determining and adjusting the scope of work. In addition, the internal auditors need access to the external auditors' management letters. Matters discussed in management letters assist internal auditors in planning the areas to emphasize in future internal audit work.

Common Understanding of Audit Techniques, Methods, and Terminology

- The CAE should understand the scope of work planned by external auditors and should be satisfied that the external auditors' planned work, in conjunction with the internal auditors' planned work, satisfies the requirements of Section 2100 of the *Standards*.

- The CAE should ensure that the external auditors' techniques, methods, and terminology are sufficiently understood by internal auditors. The CAE should also ensure that the reverse situation is taking place.

Acquisition of External Audit Services

- The internal auditor's participation in the selection, evaluation, and retention of the organization's external auditors may vary from no role in the process, to advising management or the audit committee, assistance or participation in the process, management of the process, or auditing the process. Since the IIA *Standards* require internal auditors to "share information and coordinate activities with other internal and external providers of relevant assurance and consulting services," it is advisable for internal auditors to have some role or involvement in the selection or retention of the external auditors and in the definition of scope of work.

- A board– or audit committee–approved policy can facilitate the periodic request for external audit services and position such exercises as normal business activities so that the current service providers do not view a decision to request proposals as a signal that the organization is dissatisfied with current services.

Reporting to the Board and Senior Management

Internal auditors should consider the following suggestions when reporting to the board and senior management:

- Significant engagement observations may include conditions dealing with irregularities, illegal acts, errors, inefficiency, waste, ineffectiveness, conflicts of interest, and control weaknesses.

- Management's responsibility is to make decisions on the appropriate action to be taken regarding significant engagement observations and recommendations. The CAE should consider whether it is appropriate to inform the board regarding previously reported significant observations and recommendations in those instances where senior management and the board assumed the risk of not correcting the reported condition. This may be particularly necessary where there have been changes in organization, board, senior management, or other changes.

- Activity reports should also compare (a) actual performance with the internal audit activity's goals and audit work schedules, and (b) expenditures with financial budgets. Reports should explain the reason for major variances and indicate any action taken or needed.

Relationship with the Audit Committee

Three areas of activities are key to an effective relationship between the audit committee and the internal audit function, mainly through the CAE:

1. Assisting the audit committee to ensure that its charter, activities, and processes are appropriate to fulfill its responsibilities

2. Ensuring that the charter, role, and activities of internal audit are clearly understood and responsive to the needs of the audit committee and the board

3. Maintaining open and effective communications with the audit committee and the chairperson

Internal Audit Activity's Role

The CAE's relationship to the audit committee should revolve around a core role of the CAE ensuring that the audit committee understands, supports, and receives all assistance needed from the internal audit function. The IIA supports the concept that sound governance is dependent on the synergy generated among the four principal components of effective corporate governance systems: boards of directors, management, internal auditors, and external auditors. In that structure, internal auditors and audit committees are mutually supportive.

Communications with the Audit Committee

Audit committees should:

- Meet privately with the CAE on a regular basis to discuss sensitive issues.

- Provide an annual summary report or assessment on the results of the audit activities relating to the defined mission and scope of audit work.

- Issue periodic reports to the audit committee and management summarizing results of audit activities.

- Keep the audit committee informed of emerging trends and successful practices in internal auditing.

- Discuss with the external auditor and the CAE about fulfillment of committees' information needs.

- Review information submitted to the audit committee for completeness and accuracy.

- Confirm there is effective and efficient work coordination of activities between internal and external auditors. It also should determine whether there is any duplication between the work of the internal and external auditors and give the reasons for such duplication.

Detailed Risk Assessment

Audit resources are limited and expensive, and hence they should be properly allocated and scheduled for maximum utilization. Risk models or risk analysis is often used in conjunction with development of long-range audit schedules. Performing risk analysis and risk assessment is a major step in audit planning work. A **risk** is defined as the probability that an unfavorable event occurs that could lead to a financial or other form of loss. The potential occurrence of such an event is called **exposure**. Risks are caused by exposures. Controls can reduce or eliminate risks and exposures.

Risks are inherent when business activities and transactions are processed in either a manual or an automated manner. Intentional or unintentional errors, omissions, and irregularities (e.g., theft and fraud) do occur when people handle transactions during analyzing, recording, approving, classifying, computing, processing, summarizing, posting, and reporting activities. These risks represent potentially damaging events that can produce losses.

Detailed Risk Assessment (continued)

Steps Involved in a Risk Assessment Model

- Identifying risk factors
- Judging the relative importance of the risk factors
- Measuring the extent to which each risk factor is present in an audit unit
- Quantifying and evaluating the risk level
- Allocating the audit resources according to the risk level

Audit Risk Factors

High-risk areas should receive high priority while low-risk areas should be given low priority. A systematic risk assessment approach is better than a haphazard, trial-and-error approach. Potentially important audit risk factors include:

- Quality of internal control system (most important factor)

- Competence of management

- Integrity of management

- Size of unit

- Recent change in accounting system

- Complexity of operations

- Liquidity of assets

- Recent change in key personnel

- Economic condition of unit

Audit Risk Factors (continued)

- Rapid growth

- Extent of computerized data processing

- Time since last audit

- Pressure on management to meet objectives

- Extent of government regulation

- Level of employees' morale

- Audit plans of independent auditors

- Political exposure

- Need to maintain appearance of independence by internal auditor

- Distance of unit from home office (least important factor)

Approaches to Risk Assessment

The purposes of risk analysis and assessment are to identify risks and exposures, calculate the damage or loss, and make cost-effective control recommendations. Several risk assessment techniques and approaches are available to quantify risks. Some of them, used in combination, include the following:

- Judgment and intuition
- Scoring approach
- Delphi technique
- Quantitative methods

Judgment and intuition always play an important role in risk assessment. The auditor calls on personal and professional experience and education. This is often called a gut-feel approach. Under this approach, risks may be labeled as high, medium, or low.

The **scoring approach** assigns a weight factor and a risk level to each characteristic. The product of these two numbers is the weighted risk score of the characteristic, and the sum over the risk scores of an area yields the area risk score. These areas can be ranked according to the weighted risk score.

The weight factors can be derived from using the **Delphi technique**. The audit department can use the Delphi technique to get the weights from the audit staff using their expertise in operational audits, financial audits,

Approaches to Risk Assessment (continued)

compliance audits, program audits, and computer system audits. The rationale for using the Delphi technique is that it is sometimes difficult to get a consensus on the cost or loss value and the probabilities of occurrence.

An example of a **quantitative method** involves calculating an annual loss exposure value based on estimated costs and potential losses. The annual loss exposure values are considered in the cost-effective selection of controls and safeguards. The essential elements of risk analysis are an assessment of the damage, which can be caused by an unfavorable event, and an estimate of how often such an event may happen in a period of time. Quantitative means of expressing both potential impact and estimated frequency of occurrence are necessary in performing a quantitative risk analysis. The annual loss exposure is calculated as:

$$ALE = I \times F$$

where
ALE = annual loss exposure
I = estimated impact in dollars
F = estimated frequency of occurrence per year

Approaches to Risk Assessment (continued)

Audit Risk Factors According to the IIA *Professional Standards*

These risk factors should be considered during the risk assessment process:

- Ethical climate and pressure on management to meet objectives
- Competence, adequacy, and integrity of personnel
- Asset size, liquidity, or transaction volume
- Financial and economic conditions
- Competitive conditions
- Complexity or volatility of activities
- Impact of customers, supplier, and government regulations
- Degree of computerized information systems
- Geographical dispersion of operations
- Adequacy and effectiveness of the system of internal control
- Organizational, operational, technological, or economic changes
- Management judgments and accounting estimates
- Acceptance of audit findings and corrective action taken
- Date and results of previous audits

Approaches to Risk Assessment (continued)

Risk Factors to Be Used in Conducting Risk Analysis

Factors to be used in risk analysis include (1) financial exposure and potential loss, (2) results of prior audits, and (3) major operating changes. Skills available on the audit staff is not a risk factor since missing skills can be obtained from elsewhere unless too costly that risk may be accepted.

Factors that should be considered when evaluating audit risk in a functional area include: (1) volume of transactions, (2) dollar value of "assets at risk," and (3) average value per transaction.

IIA *STANDARDS* APPLICABLE TO RISK-BASED INTERNAL AUDIT PLAN

Planning

The CAE must establish risk-based plans to determine the priorities of the internal audit activity, consistent with the organization's goals. The CAE is responsible for developing a risk-based plan. The CAE takes into account the organization's risk management framework, including using **risk appetite** levels set by management for the different activities or parts of the organization. If a framework does not exist, the CAE uses his or her own judgment of risks after consultation with senior management and the board.

The internal audit activity's plan of engagements must be based on a documented risk assessment, undertaken at least annually. The input of senior management and the board must be considered in this process.

The CAE must identify and consider the expectations of senior management, the board, and other stakeholders for internal audit opinions and other conclusions.

The CAE should consider accepting proposed consulting engagements based on the engagement's potential to improve management of risks, add value, and improve the organization's operations. Accepted engagements must be included in the plan (IIA Standard 2010).

Linking the Audit Plan to Risks and Exposures

1. In developing the internal audit activity's audit plan, many CAEs find it useful to first develop or update the audit universe. The "audit universe" is a list of all the possible audits that could be performed. The CAE may obtain input on the audit universe from senior management and the board.

2. The audit universe can include components from the organization's strategic plan. By incorporating components of the organization's strategic plan, the audit universe will consider and reflect the overall objectives of the business. Strategic plans also likely reflect the organization's attitude toward risk and the degree of difficulty to achieving planned objectives. The audit universe will normally be influenced by the results of the risk management process. The organization's strategic plan considers the environment in which the organization operates. These same environmental factors would likely impact the audit universe and assessment of relative risk.

3. The CAE prepares the internal audit activity's audit plan based on the audit universe, input from senior management and the board, and an assessment of risk and exposures affecting the organization. Key audit objectives are usually to provide senior management and the board with assurance and information to help them accomplish the organization's objectives, including an assessment of the effectiveness of management's risk management activities.

Linking the Audit Plan to Risks and Exposures (continued)

4. The audit universe and related audit plan are updated to reflect changes in management direction, objectives, emphasis, and focus. It is advisable to assess the audit universe on at least an annual basis to reflect the most current strategies and direction of the organization. In some situations, audit plans may need to be updated more frequently (e.g., quarterly) in response to changes in the organization's business, operations, programs, systems, and controls.

5. Audit work schedules are based on, among other factors, an assessment of risk and exposures. Prioritizing is needed to make decisions for applying resources. A variety of risk models exist to assist the CAE. Most risk models use risk factors such as impact, likelihood, materiality, asset liquidity, management competence, quality of and adherence to internal controls, degree of change or stability, timing and results of the last audit engagement, complexity, and employee and government relations.

Using the Risk Management Process in Internal Audit Planning

1. Risk management is a critical part of providing sound governance that touches all the organization's activities. Many organizations are moving to adopt consistent and holistic risk management approaches that should, ideally, be fully integrated into the management of the organization. It applies at all levels—enterprise, function, and business unit—of the organization. Management typically uses a risk management framework to conduct the assessment and document the assessment results.

2. An effective risk management process can assist in identifying key controls related to significant inherent risks. ERM is a term in common use. COSO of the Treadway Commission defines "ERM" as "a process, effected by an entity's board of directors, management, and other personnel, applied in strategy setting and across the enterprise, designed to identify potential events that may affect the entity, and manage risk to be within its risk appetite, to provide reasonable assurance regarding the achievement of entity objectives." Implementation of controls is one common method management can use to manage risk within its risk appetite. Internal auditors audit the key controls and provide assurance on the management of significant risks.

3. The IIA's *Standards* define "control" as "any action taken by management, the board, and other parties to manage risk and increase the likelihood that established objectives and goals will be achieved. Management plans, organizes, and directs the performance of sufficient actions to provide reasonable assurance that objectives and goals will be achieved."

Using the Risk Management Process in Internal Audit Planning (continued)

4. Two fundamental risk concepts are inherent risk and residual risk (also known as current risk). Financial/external auditors have long had a concept of inherent risk that can be summarized as the susceptibility of information or data to a material misstatement, assuming that there are no related mitigating controls. The *Standards* define "residual risk" as "the risk remaining after management takes action to reduce the impact and likelihood of an adverse event, including control activities in responding to a risk." "Current risk" is often defined as the risk managed within existing controls or control systems.

5. "Key controls" can be defined as controls or groups of controls that help to reduce an otherwise unacceptable risk to a tolerable level. Controls can be most readily conceived as organizational processes that exist to address risks. In an effective risk management process (with adequate documentation), the key controls can be readily identified from the difference between inherent and residual risk across all affected systems that are relied upon to reduce the rating of significant risks. If a rating has not been given to inherent risk, the internal auditor estimates the inherent risk rating. When identifying key controls (and assuming the internal auditor has concluded that the risk management process is mature and reliable), the internal auditor would look for:

- Individual risk factors where there is a significant reduction from inherent to residual risk (particularly if the inherent risk was very high). This highlights controls that are important to the organization.

- Controls that serve to mitigate a large number of risks.

Using the Risk Management Process in Internal Audit Planning (continued)

6. Internal audit planning needs to make use of the organizational risk management process, where one has been developed. In planning an engagement, the internal auditor considers the significant risks of the activity and the means by which management mitigates the risk to an acceptable level. The internal auditor uses risk assessment techniques in developing the internal audit activity's plan and in determining priorities for allocating internal audit resources. Risk assessment is used to examine auditable units and select areas for review to include in the internal audit activity's plan that have the greatest risk exposure.

7. Internal auditors may not be qualified to review every risk category and the ERM process in the organization (e.g., internal audits of workplace health and safety, environmental auditing, or complex financial instruments). The CAE ensures that internal auditors with specialized expertise or external service providers are used appropriately.

8. Risk management processes and systems are set up differently throughout the world. The maturity level of the organization related to risk management varies among organizations. Where organizations have a centralized risk management activity, the role of this activity includes coordinating with management regarding its continuous review of the internal control structure and updating the structure according to evolving risk appetites. The risk management processes in use in different parts of the world might have different logic, structures, and terminology. Internal auditors therefore make an assessment of the organization's risk management

Using the Risk Management Process in Internal Audit Planning (continued)

process and determine what parts can be used in developing the internal audit activity's plan and what parts can be used for planning individual internal audit assignments.

9. Factors the internal auditor considers when developing the internal audit plan include:

- Inherent risks. Are they identified and assessed?

- Residual risks. Are they identified and assessed?

- Mitigating controls, contingency plans, and monitoring activities. Are they linked to the individual events and/or risks?

- Risk registers. Are they systematic, completed, and accurate?

- Documentation. Are the risks and activities documented?

In addition, the internal auditor coordinates with other assurance providers and considers planned reliance on their work. Refer to the IIA's Practice Advisory 2050-2.

10. The internal audit charter normally requires the internal audit activity to focus on areas of high risk, including both inherent and residual risk. The internal audit activity needs to identify areas of high inherent

Using the Risk Management Process in Internal Audit Planning (continued)

risk, high residual risks, and the key control systems on which the organization is most reliant. If the internal audit activity identifies areas of unacceptable residual risk, management needs to be notified so that the risk can be addressed. The internal auditor will, as a result of conducting a strategic audit planning process, be able to identify different kinds of activities to include in the internal audit activity's plan, including:

- Control reviews/assurance activities—where the internal auditor reviews the adequacy and efficiency of the control systems and provides assurance that the controls are working and the risks are effectively managed.

- Inquiry activities—where organizational management has an unacceptable level of uncertainty about the controls related to a business activity or identified risk area and the internal auditor performs procedures to gain a better understanding of the residual risk.

- Consulting activities—where the internal auditor advises organizational management in the development of the control systems to mitigate unacceptable current risks.

Internal auditors also try to identify unnecessary, redundant, excessive, or complex controls that inefficiently reduce risk. In these cases, the cost of the control may be greater than the benefit realized. Therefore, there is an opportunity for efficiency gains in the design of the control.

Using the Risk Management Process in Internal Audit Planning (continued)

11. To ensure relevant risks are identified, the approach to risk identification is systematic and clearly documented. Documentation can range from the use of a spreadsheet in small organizations to vendor-supplied software in more sophisticated organizations. The crucial element is that the risk management framework is documented in its entirety.

12. The documentation of risk management in an organization can be at various levels below the strategic level of the risk management process. Many organizations have developed **risk registers** that document risks below the strategic level, providing documentation of significant risks in an area and related inherent and residual risk ratings, key controls, and mitigating factors. An alignment exercise can then be undertaken to identify more direct links between risk "categories" and "aspects" described in the risk registers and, where applicable, the items already included in the audit universe documented by the internal audit activity.

13. Some organizations may identify several areas of high (or higher) inherent risk. While these risks may warrant the internal audit activity's attention, it is not always possible to review all of them. Where the risk register shows a high, or above, ranking for inherent risk in a particular area, and the residual risk remains largely unchanged and no action by management or the internal audit activity is planned, the CAE reports those areas separately to the board with details of the risk analysis and reasons for the lack of, or ineffectiveness of, internal controls.

Using the Risk Management Process in Internal Audit Planning (continued)

14. A selection of lower-risk-level business unit or branch-type audits need to be included in the internal audit activity's plan periodically to give them coverage and confirm that their risks have not changed. Also, the internal audit activity establishes a method for prioritizing outstanding risks not yet subject to an internal audit.

15. An internal audit activity's plan will normally focus on:

- Unacceptable current risks where management action is required. These are areas with minimal key controls or mitigating factors that senior management wants audited immediately.

- Control systems on which the organization is most reliant.

- Areas where the differential is great between inherent risk and residual risk.

- Areas where the inherent risk is very high.

16. When planning individual internal audits, the internal auditor identifies and assesses risks relevant to the area under review.

Risk Management

The internal audit activity must evaluate the effectiveness and contribute to the improvement of risk management processes (IIA Standard 2120).

Determining whether risk management processes are effective is a judgment resulting from the internal auditor's assessment that:

- Organizational objectives support and align with the organization's mission.

- Significant risks are identified and assessed.

- Appropriate risk responses are selected that align risks with the organization's risk appetite.

- Relevant risk information is captured and communicated in a timely manner across the organization, enabling staff, management, and the board to carry out their responsibilities.

The internal audit activity may gather the information to support this assessment during multiple engagements. The results of these engagements, when viewed together, provide an understanding of the organization's risk management processes and their effectiveness.

Risk management processes are monitored through ongoing management activities, separate evaluations, or both.

Risk Management (continued)

The internal audit activity must evaluate risk exposures relating to the organization's governance, operations, and IS regarding the:

- Reliability and integrity of financial and operational information.

- Effectiveness and efficiency of operations and programs.

- Safeguarding of assets.

- Compliance with laws, regulations, policies, procedures, and contracts.

The internal audit activity must evaluate the potential for the occurrence of fraud and how the organization manages fraud risk.

During consulting engagements, internal auditors must address risk consistent with the engagement's objectives and be alert to the existence of other significant risks.

Internal auditors must incorporate knowledge of risks gained from consulting engagements into their evaluation of the organization's risk management processes.

When assisting management in establishing or improving risk management processes, internal auditors must refrain from assuming any management responsibility by actually managing risks.

Focus on: **Managing the Internal Audit Function (40–50%)**

Assessing the Adequacy of Risk Management Processes

1. Risk management is a key responsibility of senior management and the board. To achieve its business objectives, management ensures that sound risk management processes are in place and functioning. Boards have an oversight role to determine that appropriate risk management processes are in place and that these processes are adequate and effective. In this role, they may direct the internal audit activity to assist them by examining, evaluating, reporting, and/or recommending improvements to the adequacy and effectiveness of management's risk processes.

2. Management and the board are responsible for their organization's risk management and control processes. However, internal auditors acting in a consulting role can assist the organization in identifying, evaluating, and implementing risk management methodologies and controls to address those risks.

3. In situations where the organization does not have formal risk management processes, the CAE formally discusses with management and the board their obligations to understand, manage, and monitor risks within the organization and the need to satisfy themselves that there are processes operating within the organization, even if informal, that provide the appropriate level of visibility into the key risks and how they are being managed and monitored.

4. The CAE is to obtain an understanding of senior management's and the board's expectations of the internal audit activity in the organization's risk management process. This understanding is then codified in

Assessing the Adequacy of Risk Management Processes (continued)

the charters of the internal audit activity and the board. Internal auditing's responsibilities are to be coordinated between all groups and individuals within the organization's risk management process. The internal audit activity's role in the risk management process of an organization can change over time and may encompass:

- No role.

- Auditing the risk management process as part of the internal audit plan.

- Active, continuous support and involvement in the risk management process such as participation on oversight committees, monitoring activities, and status reporting.

- Managing and coordinating the risk management process.

5. Ultimately, it is the role of senior management and the board to determine the role of internal auditing in the risk management process. Their view on internal auditing's role is likely to be determined by factors such as the culture of the organization, ability of the internal audit staff, and local conditions and customs of the country. However, taking on management's responsibility regarding the risk management process and the potential threat to the internal audit activity's independence requires a full discussion and board approval.

Assessing the Adequacy of Risk Management Processes *(continued)*

6. The techniques used by various organizations for their risk management practices can vary significantly. Depending on the size and complexity of the organization's business activities, risk management processes can be:

- Formal or informal.

- Quantitative or subjective.

- Embedded in the business units or centralized at a corporate level.

7. The organization designs processes based on its culture, management style, and business objectives. For example, the use of derivatives or other sophisticated capital markets products by the organization could require the use of quantitative risk management tools. Smaller, less complex organizations could use an informal risk committee to discuss the organization's risk profile and to initiate periodic actions. The internal auditor determines that the methodology chosen is sufficiently comprehensive and appropriate for the nature of the organization's activities.

8. Internal auditors need to obtain sufficient and appropriate evidence to determine that the key objectives of the risk management processes are being met to form an opinion on the adequacy of risk management processes. In gathering such evidence, the internal auditor might consider the following audit procedures.

Assessing the Adequacy of Risk Management Processes (continued)

- Research and review current developments, trends, industry information related to the business conducted by the organization, and other appropriate sources of information to determine risks and exposures that may affect the organization and related control procedures used to address, monitor, and reassess those risks.

- Review corporate policies and board minutes to determine the organization's business strategies, risk management philosophy and methodology, appetite for risk, and acceptance of risks.

- Review previous risk evaluation reports issued by management, internal auditors, external auditors, and any other sources.

- Conduct interviews with line and senior management to determine business unit objectives, related risks, and management's risk mitigation and control monitoring activities.

- Assimilate information to independently evaluate the effectiveness of risk mitigation, monitoring, and communication of risks and associated control activities.

- Assess the appropriateness of reporting lines for risk monitoring activities.

- Review the adequacy and timeliness of reporting on risk management results.

Assessing the Adequacy of Risk Management Processes (continued)

- Review the completeness of management's risk analysis and actions taken to remedy issues raised by risk management processes, and suggest improvements.

- Determine the effectiveness of management's self-assessment processes through observations, direct tests of control and monitoring procedures, testing the accuracy of information used in monitoring activities, and other appropriate techniques.

- Review risk-related issues that may indicate weakness in risk management practices and, as appropriate, discuss with senior management and the board. If the auditor believes that management has accepted a level of risk that is inconsistent with the organization's risk management strategy and policies or that is deemed unacceptable to the organization, the auditor should refer to Standard 2600 and related guidance for additional direction.

Managing the Risk of the Internal Audit Activity

1. The role and importance of internal auditing has grown tremendously, and the expectations of key stakeholders (e.g., board, executive management) continue to expand. Internal audit activities have broad mandates to cover financial, operational, IT, legal/regulatory, and strategic risks. At the same time, many internal audit activities face challenges related to the availability of qualified personnel in the global labor markets, increased compensation costs, and high demand for specialized resources (e.g., IS, fraud, derivatives, and taxes). The combination of these factors results in a high level of risk for an internal audit activity. As a result, CAEs need to consider the risks related to their internal audit activities and the achievement of their objectives.

2. The internal audit activity is not immune to risks. It needs to take the necessary steps to ensure that it is managing its own risks.

3. Risks to internal audit activities fall into three broad categories: audit failure, false assurance, and reputation risks. The following discussion highlights the key attributes related to these risks and some steps an internal audit activity may consider to better manage them.

4. Every organization will experience control breakdowns. Often when controls fail or frauds occur, someone will ask: "Where were the internal auditors?" The internal audit activity could be a contributing factor due to:

Managing the Risk of the Internal Audit Activity (continued)

- Not following the *International Standards for the Professional Practice of Internal Auditing*.

- An inappropriate QAIP (Standard 1300), including procedures to monitor auditor independence and objectivity.

- Lack of an effective risk assessment process to identify key audit areas during the strategic risk assessment as well as areas of high risk during the planning of individual audits—as a result, failure to do the right audits and/or time wasted on the wrong audits.

- Failure to design effective internal audit procedures to test the "real" risks and the right controls.

- Failure to evaluate both the design adequacy and the control effectiveness as part of internal audit procedures.

- Use of audit teams that do not have the appropriate level of competence based on experience or knowledge of high-risk areas.

- Failure to exercise heightened professional skepticism and extended internal audit procedures related to findings or control deficiencies.

- Failure of adequate internal audit supervision.

Managing the Risk of the Internal Audit Activity (continued)

- Making the wrong decision when there was some evidence of fraud—for example, deciding "It's probably not material" or "We don't have the time or resources to deal with this issue."

- Failure to communicate suspicions to the right people.

- Failure to report adequately.

5. Internal audit failures may not only be embarrassing for internal audit activities; they also can expose an organization to significant risk. While there is no absolute assurance that audit failures will not occur, an internal audit activity can implement the following practices to mitigate such risk:

- **QAIP.** It is critical for every internal audit activity to implement an effective QAIP.

- **Periodic review of the audit universe.** Review the methodology to determine the completeness of the audit universe by routinely evaluating the organization's dynamic risk profile.

- **Periodic review of the audit plan.** Review the current audit plan to assess which assignments may be of higher risk. By flagging the higher-risk assignments, management of the internal audit activity has better visibility and may spend more time understanding the approach to the critical assignments.

Managing the Risk of the Internal Audit Activity (continued)

- **Effective planning**. There is no substitute for effective audit planning. A thorough planning process that includes updating relevant facts about the client and the performance of an effective risk assessment can significantly reduce the risks of audit failure. In addition, understanding the scope of the assignment and the internal audit procedures to be performed are important elements of the planning process that will reduce the risks of audit failure. Building internal audit activity management checkpoints into the process and obtaining approval of any deviation from the agreed-on plan is also key.

- **Effective audit design**. In most cases, a fair amount of time is spent prior to the start of testing for effectiveness in understanding and analyzing the design of the system of internal controls to determine whether it provides adequate control. Doing this provides a firm basis for internal audit comments that address root causes, which sometimes are the result of poor control design, rather than addressing symptoms. It will also reduce the chance for audit failure by identifying missing controls.

- **Effective management review and escalation procedures**. Internal audit management's involvement in the internal audit process (i.e., before the report draft) plays an important part in mitigating the risk of audit failure. This involvement might include work paper reviews, real-time discussions related to findings, or a closing meeting. By including management of the internal audit activity in the internal audit process, potential issues may be identified and assessed earlier in the assignment. In addition, an internal audit

Managing the Risk of the Internal Audit Activity (continued)

activity may have guidance procedures outlining when and what types of issues to escalate to which level of internal auditing management.

- **Proper resource allocation.** It is important to assign the right staff to each internal audit engagement. It is especially important when planning a higher-risk or a very technical engagement. Making sure the appropriate competencies are available on the team can play a significant role in reducing the risk of audit failure. In addition to the right competencies, it is important to ensure the appropriate level of experience is on the team, including strong project management skills for those leading an internal audit engagement.

6. An internal audit activity may unknowingly provide some level of false assurance. "False assurance" is a level of confidence or assurance based on perceptions or assumptions rather than fact. In many cases, the mere fact that the internal audit activity is involved in a matter may create some level of false assurance.

7. The use of internal audit resources in assisting the organization to identify and evaluate significant exposures to risk needs to be clearly defined for projects other than internal audits. For example, an internal audit activity was asked by a business unit to provide some "resources" to assist with the implementation of a new enterprise-wide computer system. The business unit deployed these resources to support some of the testing of the new system. Subsequent to the deployment, an error in the design of the system resulted in a restatement of the financial statements. When asked how this happened, the business unit responded by saying that

Managing the Risk of the Internal Audit Activity (continued)

the internal audit activity had been involved in the process and had not identified the matter. Internal audit's involvement created a level of false assurance that was not consistent with its actual role in the project.

8. While there is no way to mitigate all of the risk of false assurance, an internal audit activity can proactively manage its risk in this area. Frequent and clear communication is a key strategy to manage false assurance. Other leading practices are:

- Proactively communicate the role and the mandate of the internal audit activity to the audit committee, senior management, and other key stakeholders.

- Clearly communicate what is covered in the risk assessment, internal audit plan and internal audit engagement. Also explicitly communicate what is not in the scope of the risk assessment and internal audit plan.

- Have a "project acceptance" process to assess the level of risk related to each project and internal audit's role in the project. The assessment may consider the: scope of the project, role of the internal audit activity, reporting expectations, competencies required, and independence of internal auditors.

Managing the Risk of the Internal Audit Activity (continued)

9. If internal auditors are used to augment the staffing of a project or initiative, document their role and scope of their involvement as well as future objectivity and independence issues rather than using internal auditors as "loaned" resources, which may create false assurance. The credible reputation of an internal audit activity is an essential part of its effectiveness. Internal audit activities that are viewed with high regard are able to attract talented professionals and are highly valued by their organizations. Maintaining a strong "brand" is paramount to the internal audit activities' success and ability to contribute to the organization. In most cases, the internal audit activity's brand has been built over several years through consistent, high-quality work. Unfortunately, this brand can be destroyed instantly by one high-profile adverse event.

10. For example, an internal audit activity could be highly regarded with several of the key financial executives having had rotational assignments as internal auditors, which was viewed as a training ground for future executives. A string of significant restatements and regulatory investigations, however, would impact the reputation of the internal audit activity. The audit committee and the board might ask if the internal audit activity has the right talent and QAIP to support the organization.

11. In another example, during an audit of the human resource function, the internal auditors may discover that background checks were not being reviewed appropriately. The discovery that newly hired internal auditors

Managing the Risk of the Internal Audit Activity (continued)

did not have the appropriate education background, while others had been involved in criminal activity, could seriously impact the credibility of the internal audit activity.

12. Situations like these are not only embarrassing, but they also damage the efficacy of the internal audit activity. Protecting the reputation and the "brand" of the internal audit activity is important not only to the internal audit activity but to the entire organization. It is important that internal audit activities consider what types of risks they face that could impact their reputation and develop mitigation strategies to address these risks.

13. Some practices to protect the reputation include:

- Implement a strong QAIP over all processes in the internal audit activity, including human resources and hiring.

- Periodically perform a risk assessment for the internal audit activity to identify potential risks that might impact its brand.

Managing the Risk of the Internal Audit Activity (continued)

- Reinforce code of conduct and ethical behavior standards, including the IIA's Code of Ethics, to internal auditors.

- Ensure that the internal audit activity is in compliance with all applicable company policies and practices.

14. To the extent that an internal audit activity experiences an event outlined above, the CAE needs to review the nature of the event and gain an understanding of the root causes. This analysis provides insight into the potential changes to be considered in the internal audit process or control environment to mitigate future occurrences.

PLAN ENGAGEMENTS

Audit Process

Conducting an audit is a process with a series of activities to be reviewed and a series of procedures to be followed. A structured methodology, consisting of audit phases or stages, can be used during the audit process to ensure quality and to ensure that all required activities are accomplished—starting from the beginning of an audit to the completion of the audit. Each phase has defined tasks to be completed. Five such phases include (1) the preliminary survey, (2) the audit program, (3) fieldwork, (4) reporting, and (5) monitoring and follow-up. The audit report is the end product of the audit process.

Audit Planning

Two kinds of audit plans exist: (1) staff plans, and (2) audit plans. Staff planning should include assigning staff with the appropriate skills and knowledge for the job, assigning an adequate number of experienced staff and supervisors to the audit (consultants should be used when necessary), and providing for on-the-job training of staff.

A written audit plan should be prepared for each audit and is essential to conducting audits efficiently and effectively. The form and content of the written audit plan will vary among audits. The plan generally should include an audit program and a memorandum or other appropriate documentation of key decisions about the objectives, scope, and methodology of the audit and of the auditors' basis for those decisions.

Analytical Reviews

As a part of fieldwork, the internal auditor should perform analytical reviews to understand the relationships between various data. The focus is on determining the reasonableness of data. Techniques such as regression analysis, simple ratio analysis, and trend analysis can be used to provide insights into the financial and operational data. The outcome of the review is to provide a "red flag" to the auditor so that he or she can adjust the audit scope and the audit procedures accordingly.

Planning Materiality

Material errors, irregularities, and illegal acts will have a direct and material effect on financial statement amounts. *Materiality* is defined as the magnitude of a misstatement that would influence the judgment of a reasonable user of financial statements. Audit procedures must be designed to provide reasonable assurance of detecting material financial statement misstatements (i.e., material errors and irregularities). Thus, materiality refers to the level of precision (or accuracy) of the financial statements; the lower the materiality, the greater the precision and vice versa. From an internal audit viewpoint, materiality refers not only to the financial statements but also to the business operations and computer systems.

Types of Errors

Three types of errors can exist: (1) known errors (detected errors), (2) likely errors (estimated errors), and (3) possible errors (errors implicit in sampling work). Errors are defined as financial statement misstatements that are either intentional or unintentional.

Discovery Sampling and Errors

An auditor could use attribute sampling to estimate the percentage of checks that have problem endorsements. Attribute sampling can be used to determine the deviation rate. Variable sampling could help an auditor determine if a subunit manager of a large company had overstated an asset to increase net income and his bonus.

Discovery sampling, a special kind of attribute sampling, is very useful to fraud examiners when trying to determine whether critical errors exist. Discovery sampling allows examiners to conclude with a certain percentage confidence level whether any problem endorsements or similar critical errors exist in a population. Discovery sampling is attribute sampling with an expected error rate of zero.

Who Should Set the Materiality Level?

The auditor and the auditee should arrive at an understanding about the levels of materiality and the assurance level to be applied in an audit. This understanding should be based on cost-benefit considerations.

What Is Material and Immaterial?

Due professional care requires that the auditor consider the relative materiality or significance of matters to which audit procedures are applied. Various studies suggest that the magnitude of an error as a percentage of income is the most important factor in determining its materiality; items that have a more than 10% effect on income would normally be considered material, while items constituting less than 5% of income would normally be considered immaterial.

Qualitative versus Quantitative Materiality

Sometimes the nature of disclosure (sensitive or not) and the evidence of a desire to mislead (accidental or deliberate) are more important than quantitative factors. The auditor should weigh more toward human behavior. Quantitative materiality is applicable during the planning stage of an audit. Qualitative materiality is applicable during the evaluation stage of an audit since it is not practical to plan the audit to detect qualitative misstatements.

How to Compute Materiality

Materiality is computed by taking a base and multiplying that by a percentage. The base, in declining order of importance, includes total revenues, total expenditures, total assets, retained earnings, and income. The percentage used can be a flat percentage or one obtained from a sliding scale. A flat percentage is based on the notion that materiality is completely relative; a sliding scale is based on the notion that some amounts are large enough to be always material.

Determining Audit Objectives

Audit objectives are what the audit project is going to accomplish. Clearly defining the audit assignment objective(s) is a must at the beginning of each audit since it guides the extensiveness of internal control assessment, as well as the scope and methodology of the audit work. Audit assignments with broad objectives are generally more difficult to accomplish and require more staff resources and time than do assignments with specific objectives. Therefore, to the extent possible, audit objective(s) should be defined as precisely as possible to preclude unnecessary work, while concomitantly meeting the assignment's purpose.

Determining Audit Scope

The *scope* of an internal audit is initially defined by the audit objectives. Preliminary survey, audit programs, audit project scheduling, and time estimates are driven by audit objectives. An example of an audit objective is evaluating whether cash receipts are adequately safeguarded. Scope is the boundary of the audit. Determining the scope of the audit is part of audit planning. It addresses such things as the period and number of locations to be covered. The audit scope should include financial, operational, and compliance audits.

Considerations for Audit Scope

Determining the audit scope normally involves matters such as the number of locations to be visited, time frames to be covered, and the type and depth of work needed to ensure that assignment objectives are accomplished and that all applicable audit standards are met.

Audit Scope Impairments

During the audit engagement, auditors may find scope impairments. When factors external to the audit organization and the auditor restrict the audit scope or interfere with the auditor's ability to form objective opinions and conclusions, the auditor should attempt to remove the limitation or, failing that, report the limitation.

Audit Work Program

Preparing an *audit program* is the next step after completing the preliminary survey work. An audit program serves as a roadmap for the auditor. The audit program provides the auditor the necessary guidance to proceed with the detailed audit work in terms of audit procedures to be conducted and required audit evidence to be collected during the audit. The audit program should focus on major activities and key controls within and around such activities. Two types of audit programs exist: (1) standard audit program, and (2) customized audit program.

Audit Procedures

Audit procedures are the detailed steps, instructions, or guidelines provided for the auditor for the collection and accumulation of a particular type of audit evidence during the audit. Audit procedures can be verbal or written; the latter are preferred and are developed by auditors and approved by audit supervisors. They should be clear to enable auditors to understand what is to be accomplished.

Planning the Audit Work

Planning and managing an audit assignment starts from developing work plans to completing the audit engagement. The majority of the audit work takes place in the fieldwork phase. In planning, auditors define the audit's objectives, scope, and methodology. Planning continues throughout the audit, and auditors should document their plan and changes to it. The most important task is to make sure that sufficient staff and other resources are available to do the audit work. The audit work can be done either at the headquarters (home office) and/or at the field offices.

IIA *STANDARDS* APPLICABLE TO PLAN ENGAGEMENTS

Engagement Planning

Internal auditors must develop and document a plan for each engagement, including the engagement's objectives, scope, timing, and resource allocations (IIA Standard 2200).

1. The internal auditor plans and conducts the engagement, with supervisory review and approval. Prior to the engagement's commencement, the internal auditor prepares an engagement program that:

- States the objectives of the engagement.

- Identifies technical requirements, objectives, risks, processes, and transactions that are to be examined.

- States the nature and extent of testing required.

- Documents the internal auditor's procedures for collecting, analyzing, interpreting, and documenting information during the engagement.

- Is modified, as appropriate, during the engagement with the approval of the Chief Audit Executive (CAE), or his or her designee.

Engagement Planning (continued)

2. The CAE should require a level of formality and documentation (e.g., of the results of planning meetings, risk assessment procedures, level of detail in the work program, etc.) that is appropriate to the organization. Factors to consider would include:

- Whether the work performed and/or the results of the engagement will be relied upon by others (e.g., external auditors, regulators, or management).

- Whether the work relates to matters that may be involved in potential or current litigation.

- The experience level of the internal audit staff and the level of direct supervision required.

- Whether the project is staffed internally, by guest auditors, or by external service providers.

- The project's complexity and scope.

- The size of the internal audit activity.

- The value of documentation (e.g., whether it will be used in subsequent years).

3. The internal auditor determines the other engagement requirements, such as the period covered and estimated completion dates. The internal auditor also considers the final engagement communication format. Planning at this stage facilitates the communication process at the engagement's completion.

Engagement Planning (continued)

4. The internal auditor informs those in management who need to know about the engagement, conducts meetings with management responsible for the activity under review, summarizes and distributes the discussions and any conclusions reached from the meetings, and retains the documentation in the engagement working papers. Topics of discussion may include:

- Planned engagement objectives and scope of work.

- The resources and timing of engagement work.

- Key factors affecting business conditions and operations of the areas being reviewed, including recent changes in internal and external environment.

- Concerns or requests from management.

5. The CAE determines how, when, and to whom engagement results will be communicated. The internal auditor documents this and communicates it to management, to the extent deemed appropriate, during the planning phase of the engagement. The internal auditor communicates to management subsequent changes that affect the timing or reporting of engagement results.

Using a Top-Down, Risk-Based Approach to Identify the Controls to Be Assessed in an Internal Audit Engagement

1. Read this practice advisory in conjunction with Practice Advisories 2010-2: Using the Risk Management Process in Internal Audit Planning, 2210-1: Engagement Objectives, and 2210.A1-1: Risk Assessment in Engagement Planning and the Practice Guide GAIT for Business and IT Risk (GAIT-R).

2. This practice advisory assumes that the objectives for the internal audit engagement have been determined and the risks to be addressed have been identified in the internal audit planning process. It provides guidance on the use of a top-down, risk-based approach to identify and include in the internal audit scope (per Standard 2220) the key controls relied upon to manage the risks.

3. "Top-down" refers to basing the scope definition on the more significant risks to the organization. This is in contrast to developing the scope based on the risks at a specific location, which may not be significant to the organization as a whole. A top-down approach ensures that internal auditing is focused, as noted in Practice Advisory 2010-2, on "providing assurance on the management of significant risks."

4. A system of internal control typically includes both manual and automated controls. (Note that this applies to controls at every level — entity, business process, and information technology (IT) general controls — and in every layer of the control framework; for example, activities in the control environment, monitoring, or risk

Using a Top-Down, Risk-Based Approach to Identify the Controls to Be Assessed in an Internal Audit Engagement (continued)

assessment layers may also be automated.) Both types of controls need to be assessed to determine whether business risks are effectively managed. In particular, the internal auditor needs to assess whether there is an appropriate combination of controls, including those related to IT, to mitigate business risks within organizational tolerances. The internal auditor needs to consider including procedures to assess and confirm that risk tolerances are current and appropriate.

5. The internal audit scope needs to include all the controls required to provide reasonable assurance that the risks are effectively managed (subject to the comments in paragraph 9, below). These controls are referred to as key controls — those necessary to manage risk associated with a critical business objective. Only the key controls need to be assessed, although the internal auditor can choose to include an assessment of non-key controls (e.g., redundant, duplicative controls) if there is value to the business in providing such assurance. The internal auditor may also discuss with management whether the non-key controls are required.

6. Note that where the organization has a mature and effective risk management program, the key controls relied upon to manage each risk will have been identified. In these cases, the internal auditor needs to assess whether management's identification and assessment of the key controls is adequate.

Using a Top-Down, Risk-Based Approach to Identify the Controls to Be Assessed in an Internal Audit Engagement (continued)

7. The key controls can be in the form of:

- Entity-level controls (e.g., employees are trained and take a test to confirm their understanding of the code of conduct). The entity-level controls may be manual, fully automated, or partly automated.

- Manual controls within a business process (e.g., the performance of a physical inventory).

- Fully automated controls within a business process (e.g., matching or updating accounts in the general ledger).

- Partly automated controls within a business process (also called "hybrid" or IT-dependent controls), where an otherwise manual control relies on application functionality such as an exception report. If an error in that functionality would not be detected, the entire control could be ineffective. For example, a key control to detect duplicate payments might include the review of a system-generated report. The manual part of the control would not ensure the report is complete. Therefore, the application functionality that generated the report should be in scope.

Using a Top-Down, Risk-Based Approach to Identify the Controls to Be Assessed in an Internal Audit Engagement (continued)

The internal auditor may use other methods or frameworks, as long as all the key controls relied upon to manage the risks are identified and assessed, including manual controls, automated controls, and controls within IT general control processes.

8. Fully and partly automated controls—whether at the entity level or within a business process—generally rely on the proper design and effective operation of IT general controls. GAIT-R discusses the recommended process for identifying key IT general controls.

9. The assessment of key controls may be performed in a single, integrated internal audit engagement or in a combination of internal audit engagements. For example, one internal audit engagement may address the key controls performed by business process users, while another covers the key IT general controls, and a third assesses related controls that operate at the entity level. This is common where the same controls (especially those at the entity level or within IT general controls) are relied upon for more than one risk area.

10. As noted in paragraph 5, before providing an opinion on the effective management of the risks covered by the internal audit scope, it is necessary to assess the combination of all key controls. Even if multiple internal audit engagements are performed, each addressing some key controls, the internal auditor needs to

Using a Top-Down, Risk-Based Approach to Identify the Controls to Be Assessed in an Internal Audit Engagement (continued)

include in the scope of at least one internal audit engagement an assessment of the design of the key controls as a whole (i.e., across all the related internal audit engagements) and whether it is sufficient to manage risks within organizational tolerances.

11. If the internal audit scope (considering other internal audit engagements as discussed in paragraph 9) includes some, but not all, key controls required to manage the targeted risks, a scope limitation should be considered and clearly communicated in the internal audit notification and final report.

Planning Considerations

In planning the engagement, internal auditors must consider:

- The objectives of the activity being reviewed and the means by which the activity controls its performance;

- The significant risks to the activity, its objectives, resources, and operations and the means by which the potential impact of risk is kept to an acceptable level;

- The adequacy and effectiveness of the activity's risk management and control processes compared to a relevant control framework or model; and

- The opportunities for making significant improvements to the activity's risk management and control processes (IIA Standard 2201).

When planning an engagement for parties outside the organization, internal auditors must establish a written understanding with them about objectives, scope, respective responsibilities, and other expectations, including restrictions on distribution of the results of the engagement and access to engagement records.

Internal auditors must establish an understanding with consulting engagement clients about objectives, scope, respective responsibilities, and other client expectations. For significant engagements, this understanding must be documented.

Engagement Objectives

Objectives must be established for each engagement (IIA Standard 2210).

Internal auditors must conduct a preliminary assessment of the risks relevant to the activity under review. Engagement objectives must reflect the results of this assessment.

Internal auditors must consider the probability of significant errors, fraud, noncompliance, and other exposures when developing the engagement objectives.

Adequate criteria are needed to evaluate controls. Internal auditors must ascertain the extent to which management has established adequate criteria to determine whether objectives and goals have been accomplished. If adequate, internal auditors must use such criteria in their evaluation. If inadequate, internal auditors must work with management to develop appropriate evaluation criteria.

Consulting engagement objectives must address governance, risk management, and control processes to the extent agreed upon with the client. Consulting engagement objectives must be consistent with the organization's values, strategies, and objectives.

Establishing Engagement Objectives

1. Internal auditors establish engagement objectives to address the risks associated with the activity under review. For planned engagements, the objectives proceed and align to those initially identified during the risk assessment process from which the internal audit plan is derived. For unplanned engagements, the objectives are established prior to the start of the engagement and are designed to address the specific issue that prompted the engagement.

2. The risk assessment during the engagement's planning phase is used to further define the initial objectives and identify other significant areas of concern.

3. After identifying the risks, the auditor determines the procedures to be performed and the scope (nature, timing, and extent) of those procedures. Engagement procedures performed in appropriate scope are the means to derive conclusions related to the engagement objectives.

Risk Assessment in Engagement Planning

1. Internal auditors consider management's assessment of risks relevant to the activity under review. The internal auditor also considers:

- The reliability of management's assessment of risk.

- Management's process for monitoring, reporting, and resolving risk and control issues.

- Management's reporting of events that exceeded the limits of the organization's risk appetite and management's response to those reports.

- Risks in related activities relevant to the activity under review.

2. Internal auditors obtain or update background information about the activities to be reviewed to determine the impact on the engagement objectives and scope.

3. If appropriate, internal auditors conduct a survey to become familiar with the activities, risks, and controls to identify areas for engagement emphasis, and to invite comments and suggestions from engagement clients.

4. Internal auditors summarize the results from the reviews of management's assessment of risk, the background information, and any survey work. The summary includes:

Risk Assessment in Engagement Planning (continued)

- Significant engagement issues and reasons for pursuing them in more depth.

- Engagement objectives and procedures.

- Methodologies to be used, such as technology-based audit and sampling techniques.

- Potential critical control points, control deficiencies, and/or excess controls.

- When applicable, reasons for not continuing the engagement or for significantly modifying engagement objectives.

Engagement Scope

The established scope must be sufficient to satisfy the objectives of the engagement (IIA Standard 2220).

The scope of the engagement must include consideration of relevant systems, records, personnel, and physical properties, including those under the control of third parties.

If significant consulting opportunities arise during an assurance engagement, a specific written understanding as to the objectives, scope, respective responsibilities, and other expectations should be reached and the results of the consulting engagement communicated in accordance with consulting standards.

In performing consulting engagements, internal auditors must ensure that the scope of the engagement is sufficient to address the agreed-upon objectives. If internal auditors develop reservations about the scope during the engagement, these reservations must be discussed with the client to determine whether to continue with the engagement.

During consulting engagements, internal auditors must address controls consistent with the engagement's objectives and be alert to significant control issues.

Resource Management

The CAE must ensure that internal audit resources are appropriate, sufficient, and effectively deployed to achieve the approved plan. Appropriate refers to the mix of knowledge, skills, and other competencies needed to perform the plan. Sufficient refers to the quantity of resources needed to accomplish the plan. Resources are effectively deployed when they are used in a way that optimizes the achievement of the approved plan (IIA Standard 2030).

1. The CAE is primarily responsible for the sufficiency and management of internal audit resources in a manner that ensures the fulfillment of internal audit's responsibilities, as detailed in the internal audit charter. This includes effective communication of resource needs and reporting of status to senior management and the board. Internal audit resources may include employees, external service providers, financial support, and technology-based audit techniques. Ensuring the adequacy of internal audit resources is ultimately a responsibility of the organization's senior management and board; the CAE should assist them in discharging this responsibility.

2. The skills, capabilities, and technical knowledge of the internal audit staff are to be appropriate for the planned activities. The CAE will conduct a periodic skills assessment or inventory to determine the specific skills required to perform the internal audit activities. The skills assessment is based on and considers the various needs identified in the risk assessment and audit plan. This includes assessments of technical knowledge,

Resource Management (continued)

language skills, business acumen, fraud detection and prevention competency, and accounting and audit expertise.

3. Internal audit resources need to be sufficient to execute the audit activities in the breadth, depth, and timeliness expected by senior management and the board, as stated in the internal audit charter. Resource planning considerations include the audit universe, relevant risk levels, the internal audit plan, coverage expectations, and an estimate of unanticipated activities.

4. The CAE also ensures that resources are deployed effectively. This includes assigning auditors who are competent and qualified for specific assignments. It also includes developing a resourcing approach and organizational structure appropriate for the business structure, risk profile, and geographical dispersion of the organization.

5. From an overall resource management standpoint, the CAE considers succession planning, staff evaluation and development programs, and other human resource disciplines. The CAE also addresses the resourcing needs of the internal audit activity, whether those skills are present or not within the internal audit activity itself. Other approaches to addressing resource needs include external service providers, employees from other departments within the organization, or specialized consultants.

Resource Management (continued)

6. Because of the critical nature of resources, the CAE maintains ongoing communications and dialog with senior management and the board on the adequacy of resources for the internal audit activity. The CAE periodically presents a summary of status and adequacy of resources to senior management and the board. To that end, the CAE develops appropriate metrics, goals, and objectives to monitor the overall adequacy of resources. This can include comparisons of resources to the internal audit plan, the impact of temporary shortages or vacancies, educational and training activities, and changes to specific skill needs based on changes in the organization's business, operations, programs, systems, and controls.

Engagement Resource Allocation

Internal auditors must determine appropriate and sufficient resources to achieve engagement objectives based on an evaluation of the nature and complexity of each engagement, time constraints, and available resources (IIA Standard 2230).

Internal auditors consider the following when determining the appropriateness and sufficiency of resources:

- The number and experience level of the internal audit staff.

- Knowledge, skills, and other competencies of the internal audit staff when selecting internal auditors for the engagement.

- Availability of external resources where additional knowledge and competencies are required.

- Training needs of internal auditors as each engagement assignment serves as a basis for meeting the internal audit activity's developmental needs.

Engagement Work Program

Internal auditors must develop and document work programs that achieve the engagement objectives (IIA Standard 2240).

1. Work programs must include the procedures for identifying, analyzing, evaluating, and documenting information during the engagement. The work program must be approved prior to its implementation, and any adjustments approved promptly.

2. Work programs for consulting engagements may vary in form and content depending upon the nature of the engagement.

3. Internal auditors develop and obtain documented approval of work programs before commencing the internal audit engagement. The work program includes methodologies to be used, such as technology-based audit and sampling techniques.

4. The process of collecting, analyzing, interpreting, and documenting information is to be supervised to provide reasonable assurance that engagement objectives are met and that the internal auditor's objectivity is maintained.

SUPERVISE ENGAGEMENTS

Audit Scheduling

An audit schedule is an essential part of planning internal auditing department activities. Since audit resources, in terms of available time and the number of auditors, are limited, the audit manager needs to balance the needs of the audit plan and the availability of resources. It is prudent to hire auditors with different skill and experience levels so that all required skills are available among the audit staff even though each auditor may not have all the required skills.

Audit Supervision

Assigning and using staff is important to satisfying audit objectives. Since skills and knowledge vary among auditors, work assignments must be commensurate with skills and abilities.

Supervisors should satisfy themselves that staff members clearly understand their assigned tasks before starting the work. Staff should be informed not only of what work they are to do and how they are to proceed, but also why the work is to be conducted and what it is expected to accomplish. With experienced staff, the supervisors' role may be more general. They may outline the scope of the work and leave details to assistants. With a less experienced staff, a supervisor may have to specify not only how to gather data but also techniques for analyzing them.

Effective supervision ensures that audit assignments are properly planned and produce a high-quality and consistent product. A competent supervisor can help in preparing audit plans, developing and controlling budgets and schedules, improving auditor and auditee relationships, ensuring the preparation of consistent and quality working papers, and reviewing audit reports.

Collecting Data and Information

Since management makes decisions and auditors use information, they need to know how and where the information is coming from. At least four sources of information are available: primary and secondary information and internal and external sources.

Managers should think of problems and opportunities as information needs, as a series of questions that need to be answered. *Information consciousness means to think information when thinking about problems.*

Evaluating the Audit Evidence

Evaluating the audit evidence includes knowing the types of audit evidence to be considered, understanding the standards of audit evidence, and using the audit evidence appropriately.

Types of Audit Evidence

Audit evidence is information that provides a factual basis for audit opinions. It is the information documented by the auditors and obtained through observing conditions, interviewing people, examining records, and testing documents. Audit evidence may be categorized as physical, documentary, testimonial, and analytical.

Standards of Audit Evidence

All audit evidence should meet the three standards of sufficiency, competence, and relevance. Evidence is sufficient if it is based on facts. Competent evidence is reliable evidence. The term "relevance" refers to the relationship of the information to its use. When audit evidence does not meet these three standards, additional (corroborative) evidence is required before expressing an audit opinion.

Appropriateness of Audit Evidence

The phrase "appropriateness of audit evidence" refers to persuasiveness (sufficiency), relevance (consistency), and competence (reliability).

Information Sources for Audit Evidence

The auditors' approach to determining the sufficiency, relevance, and competence of evidence depends on the source of the information that constitutes the evidence. Information sources include original data gathered by auditors and existing data gathered by either the auditee or a third party. Data may also be obtained from computer-based systems.

Develop and Review Audit Working Papers

Working papers are the link between fieldwork and the audit report. The requirements to prepare working papers may be satisfied with documentation maintained on disks, tapes, or film. Working papers serve three purposes: (1) they provide the principal support for the auditors' report, (2) they aid the auditors in conducting and supervising the audit, and (3) they allow others to review the audit's quality.

Working papers should contain:

- Objective, scope, and methodology, including any sampling criteria used, and results of the audit

- Evidence of the work performed to support findings, judgments, and conclusions

- Evidence of supervisory reviews of the work conducted

IIA *STANDARDS* APPLICABLE TO SUPERVISE ENGAGEMENTS

Performing the Engagement

Internal auditors must identify, analyze, evaluate, and document sufficient information to achieve the engagement's objectives (IIA Standard 2300).

Use of Personal Information in Conducting Engagements

1. Internal auditors need to consider concerns relating to the protection of personally identifiable information gathered during audit engagements as advances in information technology and communications continue to present privacy risks and threats. Privacy controls are legal requirements in many jurisdictions.

2. Personal information generally refers to data associated with a specific individual or data that has identifying characteristics that may be combined with other information. It includes any factual or subjective information, recorded or not, in any form or media. Personal information includes:

- Name, address, identification numbers, income, blood type.

- Evaluations, social status, disciplinary actions.

- Employee files and credit and loan records.

- Employee health and medical data.

3. In many jurisdictions, laws require organizations to identify the purposes for which personal information is collected at or before the time of collection. These laws also prohibit using and disclosing personal information for purposes other than those for which it was collected except with the individual's consent or as required by law.

Use of Personal Information in Conducting Engagements (continued)

4. It is important that internal auditors understand and comply with all laws regarding the use of personal information in their jurisdiction and in those jurisdictions where their organizations conduct business.

5. It may be inappropriate, and in some cases illegal, to access, retrieve, review, manipulate, or use personal information in conducting certain internal audit engagements. If the internal auditor accesses personal information, it may be necessary to develop procedures to safeguard this information. For example, the internal auditor may decide not to record personal information in engagement records in some situations.

6. The internal auditor may seek advice from legal counsel before beginning audit work if there are questions or concerns about access to personal information.

Identifying Information

Internal auditors must identify sufficient, reliable, relevant, and useful information to achieve the engagement's objectives. Sufficient information is factual, adequate, and convincing so that a prudent, informed person would reach the same conclusions as the auditor. Reliable information is the best attainable information through the use of appropriate engagement techniques. Relevant information supports engagement observations and recommendations and is consistent with the objectives for the engagement. Useful information helps the organization meet its goals (IIA Standard 2310).

Analysis and Evaluation

Internal auditors must base conclusions and engagement results on appropriate analyses and evaluations (IIA Standard 2320).

1. Internal auditors may use analytical procedures to obtain audit evidence. Analytical procedures involve studying and comparing relationships among both financial and nonfinancial information. The application of analytical procedures is based on the premise that, in the absence of known conditions to the contrary, relationships among information may reasonably be expected to exist and continue. Examples of contrary conditions include unusual or nonrecurring transactions or events; accounting, organizational, operational, environmental, and technological changes; inefficiencies; ineffectiveness; errors; fraud; or illegal acts.

2. Analytical procedures often provide the internal auditor with an efficient and effective means of obtaining evidence. The assessment results from comparing information with expectations identified or developed by the internal auditor. Analytical procedures are useful in identifying:

- Unexpected differences.

- The absence of differences when they are expected.

- Potential errors.

Analysis and Evaluation (continued)

- Potential fraud or illegal acts.

- Other unusual or nonrecurring transactions or events.

  3. Analytical audit procedures include:

- Comparing current period information with expectations based on similar information for prior periods as well as budgets or forecasts.

- Studying relationships between financial and appropriate nonfinancial information (e.g., recorded payroll expense compared to changes in average number of employees).

- Studying relationships among elements of information (e.g., fluctuation in recorded interest expense compared to changes in related debt balances).

- Comparing information with expectations based on similar information for other organizational units as well as for the industry in which the organization operates.

  4. Internal auditors may perform analytical procedures using monetary amounts, physical quantities, ratios, or percentages. Specific analytical procedures include ratio, trend, and regression analysis; reasonableness

Analysis and Evaluation (continued)

tests; period-to-period comparisons; comparisons with budgets; forecasts; and external economic information. Analytical procedures assist internal auditors in identifying conditions that may require additional audit procedures. An internal auditor uses analytical procedures in planning the engagement in accordance with the guidelines contained in Standard 2200.

5. Internal auditors may use analytical procedures to generate evidence during the audit engagement. When determining the extent of analytical procedures, the internal auditor considers the:

- Significance of the area being audited.

- Assessment of risk management in the area being audited.

- Adequacy of the internal control system.

- Availability and reliability of financial and nonfinancial information.

- Precision with which the results of analytical audit procedures can be predicted.

- Availability and comparability of information regarding the industry in which the organization operates.

- Extent to which other procedures provide evidence.

Analysis and Evaluation (continued)

6. When analytical audit procedures identify unexpected results or relationships, the internal auditor evaluates such results or relationships. This evaluation includes determining whether the difference from expectations could be a result of fraud, error, or a change in conditions. The auditor may ask management about the reasons for the difference and would corroborate management's explanation, for example, by modifying expectations and recalculating the difference or by applying other audit procedures. In particular, the internal auditor needs to be satisfied that the explanation considers both the direction of the change (e.g., sales decreased) and the amount of the difference (e.g., sales decreased by 10 percent). Unexplained results or relationships from applying analytical procedures may be indicative of a significant problem (e.g., a potential error, fraud, or illegal act). Results or relationships that are not adequately explained may indicate a situation to be communicated to senior management and the board in accordance with Standard 2060. Depending on the circumstances, the internal auditor may recommend appropriate action.

Documenting Information

Internal auditors must document relevant information to support the conclusions and engagement results (IIA Standard 2330).

The CAE must control access to engagement records. The chief audit executive must obtain the approval of senior management and/or legal counsel prior to releasing such records to external parties, as appropriate.

The CAE must develop retention requirements for engagement records, regardless of the medium in which each record is stored. These retention requirements must be consistent with the organization's guidelines and any pertinent regulatory or other requirements.

The CAE must develop policies governing the custody and retention of consulting engagement records, as well as their release to internal and external parties. These policies must be consistent with the organization's guidelines and any pertinent regulatory or other requirements.

Audit Working Papers

1. Internal auditors prepare working papers. Working papers document the information obtained, the analyses made, and the support for the conclusions and engagement results. Internal audit management reviews the prepared working papers.

2. Engagement working papers generally:

- Aid in the planning, performance, and review of engagements.

- Provide the principal support for engagement results.

- Document whether engagement objectives were achieved.

- Support the accuracy and completeness of the work performed.

- Provide a basis for the internal audit activity's quality assurance and improvement program.

- Facilitate third-party reviews.

3. The organization, design, and content of engagement working papers depend on the engagement's nature and objectives and the organization's needs. Engagement working papers document all aspects of the

Audit Working Papers (continued)

engagement process from planning to communicating results. The internal audit activity determines the media used to document and store working papers.

4. The CAE establishes working paper policies for the various types of engagements performed. Standardized engagement working papers, such as questionnaires and audit programs, may improve the engagement's efficiency and facilitate the delegation of engagement work. Engagement working papers may be categorized as permanent or carry-forward engagement files that contain information of continuing importance.

Control of Engagement Records

1. Internal audit engagement records include reports, supporting documentation, review notes, and correspondence, regardless of storage media. Engagement records or working papers are the property of the organization. The internal audit activity controls engagement working papers and provides access to authorized personnel only.

2. Internal auditors may educate management and the board about access to engagement records by external parties. Policies relating to access to engagement records, handling of access requests, and procedures to be followed when an engagement warrants an investigation, need to be reviewed by the board.

3. Internal audit policies explain who in the organization is responsible for ensuring the control and security of the activity's records, which internal or external parties can be granted access to engagement records, and how requests for access to those records need to be handled. These policies will vary depending on the nature of the organization, practices followed in the industry, and access privileges established by law.

4. Management and other members of the organization may request access to all or specific engagement working papers. Such access may be necessary to substantiate or explain engagement observations and recommendations or for other business purposes. The CAE approves these requests.

5. The CAE approves access to engagement working papers by external auditors.

Control of Engagement Records (continued)

6. There are circumstances where parties outside the organization, other than external auditors, request access to engagement working papers and reports. Prior to releasing the documentation, the CAE obtains the approval of senior management and/or legal counsel, as appropriate.

7. Potentially, internal audit records that are not specifically protected may be accessed in legal proceedings. Legal requirements vary significantly in different jurisdictions. When there is a specific request for engagement records in relation to a legal proceeding, the CAE works closely with legal counsel in deciding what to provide.

Granting Access to Engagement Records

Caution: Internal auditors are encouraged to consult legal counsel in matters involving legal issues as requirements may vary significantly in different jurisdictions. The guidance contained in this practice advisory is based primarily on the legal systems that protect information and work performed for, or communicated to, an engaged attorney (i.e., attorney–client privilege), such as the legal system in the United States of America.

1. Internal audit engagement records include reports, supporting documentation, review notes, and correspondence, regardless of storage media. Engagement records are generally produced under the presumption that their contents are confidential and may contain a mix of facts and opinions. However, those who are not familiar with the organization or its internal audit process may misunderstand those facts and opinions. Outside parties may seek access to engagement records in different types of proceedings, including criminal prosecutions, civil litigation, tax audits, regulatory reviews, government contract reviews, and reviews by self-regulatory organizations. Most of an organization's records that are not protected by the attorney–client privilege may be accessible in criminal proceedings. In noncriminal proceedings, the issue of access is less clear and may vary according to the jurisdiction of the organization.

2. Explicit practices of the internal audit activity may increase the control of access to engagement records.

3. The internal audit activity may address access to, and control of, internal audit records regardless of the media used for storage.

Granting Access to Engagement Records (continued)

4. The internal audit activity's policies should cover what to include in engagement records and specify the content and format of the engagement records and how internal auditors handle resolved review notes. The policies also should specify how long internal audit records are to be retained. The CAE, when specifying the length of retention for engagement records, should consider the organization's needs as well as legal requirements.

5. The internal audit activity's policies may document who in the organization is responsible for the control and security of internal audit records, who can be granted access to engagement records, and how requests for access to those records are to be handled. These policies depend on the practices followed in the organization's industry or legal jurisdiction. The CAE should be aware of changing practices in the industry and changing legal precedents. When developing policies, the CAE should consider who may seek access to internal audit records.

6. The policy granting access to engagement records may also address processes:

- For resolving access issues.

- For educating the internal audit staff concerning the risks and issues regarding access to their work products.

- To determine who may seek access to the work product in the future.

Granting Access to Engagement Records (continued)

7. The CAE also may educate senior management and the board about the risks of access to engagement records. The board may review policies relating to who can be granted access to engagement records and how those requests are to be handled. The specific policies will vary depending upon the nature of the organization and the access privileges that have been established by law.

8. When furnishing engagement records, the CAE usually:

- Provides only the specific documents as directed by legal counsel or policies. These usually exclude documents covered by attorney–client privilege. Documents that reveal attorneys' thought processes or strategies will usually be privileged and not subject to forced disclosure.

- Releases documents in a form where they cannot be changed (e.g., as an image rather than in word processing format). For paper documents, the CAE releases copies and keeps the originals.

- Labels each document as confidential and places a notation that secondary distribution is not permitted without permission.

Retention of Records

1. Engagement record retention requirements vary among jurisdictions and legal environments.

2. The CAE develops a written retention policy that meets organizational needs and legal requirements of the jurisdictions within which the organization operates.

3. The record retention policy needs to include appropriate arrangements for the retention of records related to engagements performed by external service providers.

Engagement Supervision

Engagements must be properly supervised to ensure objectives are achieved, quality is assured, and staff is developed. The extent of supervision required will depend on the proficiency and experience of internal auditors and the complexity of the engagement. The CAE has overall responsibility for supervising the engagement, whether performed by or for the internal audit activity, but may designate appropriately experienced members of the internal audit activity to perform the review. Appropriate evidence of supervision is documented and retained (IIA Standard 2340).

1. The CAE or designee provides appropriate engagement supervision. Supervision is a process that begins with planning and continues throughout the engagement. The process includes:

- Ensuring designated auditors collectively possess the required knowledge, skills, and other competencies to perform the engagement.

- Providing appropriate instructions during the planning of the engagement and approving the engagement program.

- Ensuring the approved engagement program is completed unless changes are justified and authorized.

- Determining engagement working papers adequately support engagement observations, conclusions, and recommendations.

Engagement Supervision (continued)

- Ensuring engagement communications are accurate, objective, clear, concise, constructive, and timely.

- Ensuring engagement objectives are met.

- Providing opportunities for developing internal auditors' knowledge, skills, and other competencies.

2. The CAE is responsible for all internal audit engagements, whether performed by or for the internal audit activity, and all significant professional judgments made throughout the engagement. The CAE also adopts suitable means to ensure this responsibility is met. Suitable means include policies and procedures designed to:

- Minimize the risk that internal auditors or others performing work for the internal audit activity make professional judgments or take other actions that are inconsistent with the CAE's professional judgment such that the engagement is impacted adversely.

- Resolve differences in professional judgment between the CAE and internal audit staff over significant issues relating to the engagement. Such means may include discussion of pertinent facts, further inquiry or research, and documentation and disposition of the differing viewpoints in engagement working papers. In instances of a difference in professional judgment over an ethical issue, suitable means may include referral of the issue to those individuals in the organization having responsibility over ethical matters.

Engagement Supervision (continued)

3. All engagement working papers are reviewed to ensure they support engagement communications and necessary audit procedures are performed. Evidence of supervisory review consists of the reviewer initialing and dating each working paper after it is reviewed. Other techniques that provide evidence of supervisory review include completing an engagement working paper review checklist; preparing a memorandum specifying the nature, extent, and results of the review; or evaluating and accepting reviews within the working paper software.

4. Reviewers can make a written record (i.e., review notes) of questions arising from the review process. When clearing review notes, care needs to be taken to ensure working papers provide adequate evidence that questions raised during the review are resolved. Alternatives with respect to disposition of review notes are as follow:

- Retain the review notes as a record of the reviewer's questions raised, the steps taken in their resolution, and the results of those steps.

- Discard the review notes after the questions raised are resolved and the appropriate engagement working papers are amended to provide the information requested.

5. Engagement supervision also allows for training and development of staff and performance evaluation.

COMMUNICATE ENGAGEMENT RESULTS

Audit Report Purpose and Timeliness

Written audit reports serve multiple purposes. They communicate the results of the audit work to auditees and others, make the results less susceptible to misunderstanding, and facilitate follow-up reviews to determine whether appropriate corrective actions have been taken.

To be of maximum use, the audit report must be timely. A carefully prepared report may be of little value to decision makers if it arrives too late. Therefore, the audit organization should plan for the prompt issuance of the audit report and conduct the audit with this goal in mind.

The auditors should consider interim reporting, during the audit, of significant matters to appropriate auditees. Such communication, which may be oral or written, is not a substitute for a final written report, but it does alert auditees to matters needing immediate attention and permits them to correct the problems before the final report is completed.

Audit Report Contents

The contents of an audit report include audit objectives; audit scope; audit methodology used; compliance with standards, regulations, and laws; management responses; noteworthy accomplishments of management; and deficiency audit findings, including recommendations.

Objectives, Scope, and Methodology

Readers need knowledge of the objectives of the audit, as well as the audit scope and methodology for achieving the objectives, to understand the purpose of audit, judge the merits of the audit work and what is reported, and understand any significant limitations.

Compliance with Standards, Regulations, and Laws

The statement of conformity refers to the applicable standards that the auditors should have followed during the audit. The statement need not be qualified when standards that were not applicable were not followed. When applicable standards were not followed, the auditors should modify the statement to disclose in the scope section of their report the required standard that was not followed, why, and the known effect that not following the standard had on the results of the audit.

Management Responses

One of the most effective ways to ensure that a report is fair, complete, and objective is to obtain advance review and comments by responsible auditee (management) and others, as may be appropriate. Including the views of the auditee produces a report that shows not only what was found and what the auditors think about it, but also what the responsible persons think about it and what they plan to do about it.

Noteworthy Accomplishments of Management

Significant management accomplishments identified during the audit that were within the scope of the audit should be included in the audit report, along with deficiencies.

Desirable Attributes of a Deficiency Audit Finding

Audit findings have often been regarded as containing the elements of criteria, condition, and effect, plus cause when problems are found. However, the elements needed for a finding depend entirely on the objectives of the audit. This means the elements "cause" and "effect" may be optional for a compliance audit, but they are musts for an operational audit. Thus, a finding or set of findings is complete to the extent that the audit objectives are satisfied and the report clearly relates those objectives to the finding's elements. A deficiency audit finding should have four elements or attributes, with a recommendation as optional (i.e., criteria, condition, cause, effect, and recommendation).

○ **Criteria** are the standards used to determine whether an operation, function, or program meets or exceeds expectations. Criteria provide a context for understanding the results of the audit. The audit plan, where possible, should state the criteria to be used. In selecting criteria, auditors have a responsibility to use only criteria that are reasonable, attainable, and relevant to the matters being audited. When the criteria are vague, the auditors should seek interpretation. If interpretation is not available, auditors should strive to agree on the appropriateness of these measures with the interested parties or, if applicable, indicate that they were unable to report on performance because of the lack of definite criteria. It represents "what should be" at the time of the audit.

○ **Condition** is a situation that exists. It has been observed and documented during the audit. It represents "what is" at the time of the audit.

○ **Cause** has two meanings, which depend on the audit objectives. When the auditors' objective is to explain why the poor (or good) performance observed in the audit happened, the reasons for the observed

Desirable Attributes of a Deficiency Audit Finding (continued)

performance are referred to as "cause." Identifying the cause of problems is necessary before making constructive recommendations for correction. Because problems can result from a number of plausible factors, auditors need to clearly demonstrate and explain with evidence and reasoning the link between the problems and the factor(s) they identified as the cause. When the auditors' objective includes estimating the impact of a program on changes in physical, social, or economic conditions, they seek evidence of the extent to which the program itself is the "cause" of those changes.

○ **Effect** also has two meanings, which depend on the audit objectives. When the auditors' objectives include identifying the actual or potential consequences of a condition that varies (either positively or negatively) from the criteria identified in the audit, "effect" is a measure of those consequences. Auditors often use effect in this sense to demonstrate the need for corrective action in response to identified problems. When the auditors' objectives include estimating the effectiveness of an operation or a program in causing changes in physical, social, or economic conditions, "effect" is a measure of the impact achieved by the operation or program. Here effect is the extent to which positive or negative changes in actual physical, social, or economic conditions can be identified and attributed to program or operations.

○ **Recommendations** state what an audit organization believes should be done to accomplish beneficial results. They do not direct what must be done but seek to convince others (e.g., the auditee) of what needs to be done. Recommendations should be action-oriented, convincing, well supported, and effective. When appropriately implemented, they should get the desired beneficial results.

Audit Report Presentation and Distribution

The audit report should be complete, accurate, objective, convincing, and as clear and concise as the subject permits.

○ **Complete**. Being complete requires that the report contain all information needed to satisfy the audit objectives, promote an adequate and correct understanding of the matters reported, and meet the applicable report content requirements. It also means including appropriate background information.

Giving readers an adequate and correct understanding means providing perspective on the extent and significance of reported findings, such as frequency of occurrence relative to the number of cases or transactions tested and the relationship of the findings to the entity's operations.

Except as necessary to make convincing presentations, detailed supporting data need not be included. In most cases, a single example of a deficiency is not sufficient to support a broad conclusion or a related recommendation. All that it supports is that there was a deviation, an error, or a control weakness.

○ **Accurate**. Accuracy requires that the evidence presented be true and that findings be correctly portrayed. The need for accuracy is based on the need to assure readers that what it reported is credible and reliable. One inaccuracy in a report can cast doubt on the validity of an entire report and can divert attention from its substance. Also, inaccurate reports can damage the credibility of the issuing audit organization and reduce the effectiveness of reports it issues.

Audit Report Presentation and Distribution (continued)

The report should include only information, findings, and conclusions that are supported by competent and relevant evidence in the auditors' working papers. That evidence should demonstrate the correctness and reasonableness of the matters reported. The term "correct portrayal" means describing accurately the audit scope and methodology, and presenting findings and conclusions in a manner consistent with the scope of audit work.

○ **Objective**. Objectivity requires that the presentation of the entire report be balanced in content and tone. A report's credibility is significantly enhanced when it presents evidence in an unbiased manner so that readers can be persuaded by the facts.

The audit report should be fair and not be misleading, and should place the audit results in proper perspective. This means presenting the audit results impartially and guarding against the tendency to exaggerate or overemphasize deficient performance. In describing shortcomings in performance, auditors should present the explanation of responsible auditees, including the consideration of any unusual difficulties or circumstances they faced.

The tone of reports should encourage favorable reaction to findings and recommendations. Titles, captions, and the text of reports should be stated constructively. Although findings should be presented clearly and forthrightly, the auditors should keep in mind that one of their objectives is to persuade and that this can best be done by avoiding language that generates defensiveness and opposition. Although criticism of past performance is often necessary, the report should emphasize needed improvements.

○ **Convincing**. Being convincing requires that the audit results are responsive to the audit objectives, the findings are presented persuasively, and the conclusions and recommendations follow logically from the facts presented. The information presented should be sufficient to enable the readers of the validity of the findings,

2

Audit Report Presentation and Distribution (continued)

the reasonableness of the conclusions, and the desirability of implementing the recommendations. Reports designed in this way can help focus the attention of management on the matters that warrant attention and can help stimulate correction.

○ **Clear**. Clarity requires that the report be easy to read and understand. Reports should be written in language as clear and simple as the subject permits. Use of straightforward, nontechnical language is essential to simplicity of presentation. If technical terms and unfamiliar abbreviations and acronyms are used, they should be clearly defined. Acronyms should be used sparingly.

Both logical organization of material and accuracy and precision in stating facts and in drawing conclusions are essential to clarity and understanding. Effective use of titles and captions and topic sentences make the report easier to read and understand. Visual aids (i.e., pictures, charts, graphs, and diagrams) should be used when appropriate to clarify and summarize complex material.

○ **Concise**. Being concise requires that the report be no longer than necessary to convey the message. Too much detail detracts from a report, may even conceal the real message, and may confuse or discourage readers. Also, needless repetition should be avoided. Although room exists for considerable judgment in determining the content of reports, those that are complete but still concise are likely to receive greater attention.

Final Audit Report

The final report should be distributed to auditees directly interested in the audit work results and those responsible for acting on the findings and recommendations. Higher-level members in the organization may receive only a summary report. Reports may also be distributed to other interested or affected parties, such as external auditors and the board of directors.

Certain information may not be appropriate for disclosure to all report recipients because it is privileged, proprietary, or related to improper or illegal acts. Such information, however, may be disclosed in a separate report. If the conditions being reported involve senior management, report distribution should be to the board of the organization.

Oral and Written Audit Reports

In some circumstances, it might be appropriate for auditors to issue oral reports. If they issue an oral report, the auditors should keep a written record of what they communicated and the basis for not issuing a written report. An oral report may be most appropriate when emergency action is needed. Before issuing an oral report, auditors should determine that both of these conditions exist

1. An oral report would effectively meet decision makers' needs for information about the results of the audit.

2. It is unlikely that parties other than those who would receive the oral report would have a significant interest in the results of the audit.

Written audit reports in a summary form (summary reports) are generally intended for high-level management and/or the audit committee. However, a detailed audit report dealing with payroll department with significant control weaknesses should be most useful to the payroll department manager.

Benefits of Audit Work

Four basic principles to ensure the benefits of the audit work include (1) quality recommendations, (2) commitment, (3) monitoring and follow-up system, and (4) special attention to key recommendations.

IIA *STANDARDS* APPLICABLE TO COMMUNICATE ENGAGEMENT RESULTS

Communicating Results

Internal auditors must communicate the results of engagements (IIA Standard 2400).

Legal Considerations in Communicating Results

Caution: Internal auditors are encouraged to consult legal counsel in matters involving legal issues as requirements may vary significantly in different jurisdictions. The guidance contained in this practice advisory is based primarily on the legal systems that protect information and work performed for, or communicated to, an engaged attorney (i.e., attorney–client privilege), such as the legal system in the United States of America.

1. The internal auditor needs to exercise caution when communicating noncompliance with laws, regulations, and other legal issues. Developing policies and procedures regarding the handling of those matters as well as a close working relationship with other appropriate areas (e.g., legal counsel and compliance) is strongly encouraged.

2. The internal auditor gathers evidence, makes analytical judgments, reports results, and determines whether management has taken appropriate corrective action. The internal auditor's need to prepare engagement records may conflict with legal counsel's desire to not leave discoverable evidence that could harm the organization's position in legal matters. For example, even if an internal auditor gathers and evaluates information properly, the facts and analyses disclosed may negatively impact the organization from a legal perspective. Proper planning and policy making — including role definition and methods of communication — are essential so that a sudden revelation does not place the internal auditor and legal counsel at odds with one another. Both parties need to foster an ethical and preventive perspective throughout the organization by sensitizing and educating management about the established policies.

Legal Considerations in Communicating Results (continued)

3. A communication made between "privileged persons" — in confidence and for the purpose of seeking, obtaining, or providing legal assistance for the client — is necessary to protect the attorney–client privilege. This privilege, which is primarily used to protect communications with attorneys, can also apply to communications with third parties working with an attorney.

4. Some courts have recognized a privilege of critical self-analysis that shields self-critical materials (e.g., audit work products) from discovery. In general, the recognition of this privilege is premised on the belief that the confidentiality of the self-analysis in these instances outweighs the valued public interest.

5. Privilege usually applies when:

- The information results from a self-critical analysis undertaken by the party asserting the privilege.

- The public has a strong interest in preserving the free flow of the information contained in the critical analysis.

- The information is of the type whose flow would be curtailed if discovery were allowed.

Legal Considerations in Communicating Results (continued)

6. Self-evaluative privileges are less likely to be available when a government agency — rather than a party involved in a private legal matter — seeks out the documents. Presumably, this reluctance results from recognition of the government's stronger interest in enforcing the law.

7. Documents intended to be protected under the work-product doctrine usually need to be:

- Some type of work product (e.g., memo, computer program).

- Prepared in anticipation of litigation.

- Completed by someone working at the direction of an attorney.

8. Documents prepared and delivered to the attorney before the attorney–client relationship is established are not generally protected by the attorney–client privilege.

Criteria for Communicating

Communications must include the engagement's objectives and scope as well as applicable conclusions, recommendations, and action plans (IIA Standard 2410).

Final communication of engagement results must, where appropriate, contain the internal auditors' opinion and/or conclusions. When issued, an opinion or conclusion must take account of the expectations of senior management, the board, and other stakeholders and must be supported by sufficient, reliable, relevant, and useful information.

Opinions at the engagement level may be ratings, conclusions, or other descriptions of the results. Such an engagement may be in relation to controls around a specific process, risk, or business unit. The formulation of such opinions requires consideration of the engagement results and their significance.

Internal auditors are encouraged to acknowledge satisfactory performance in engagement communications.

When releasing engagement results to parties outside the organization, the communication must include limitations on distribution and use of the results.

Communication of the progress and results of consulting engagements will vary in form and content depending upon the nature of the engagement and the needs of the client.

1. Although the format and content of the final engagement communications varies by organization or type of engagement, they are to contain, at a minimum, the purpose, scope, and results of the engagement.

Criteria for Communicating (continued)

2. Final engagement communications may include background information and summaries. Background information may identify the organizational units and activities reviewed and provide explanatory information. It may also include the status of observations, conclusions, and recommendations from prior reports and an indication of whether the report covers a scheduled engagement or is responding to a request. Summaries are balanced representations of the communication's content.

3. Purpose statements describe the engagement objectives and may inform the reader why the engagement was conducted and what it was expected to achieve.

4. Scope statements identify the audited activities and may include supportive information such as time period reviewed and related activities not reviewed to delineate the boundaries of the engagement. They may describe the nature and extent of engagement work performed.

5. Results include observations, conclusions, opinions, recommendations, and action plans.

6. Observations are pertinent statements of fact. The internal auditor communicates those observations necessary to support or prevent misunderstanding of the internal auditor's conclusions and recommendations. The internal auditor may communicate less significant observations or recommendations informally.

Criteria for Communicating (continued)

7. Engagement observations and recommendations emerge by a process of comparing criteria (the correct state) with condition (the current state). Whether or not there is a difference, the internal auditor has a foundation on which to build the report. When conditions meet the criteria, communication of satisfactory performance may be appropriate. Observations and recommendations are based on the following attributes:

- **Criteria:** The standards, measures, or expectations used in making an evaluation and/or verification (the correct state).

- **Condition:** The factual evidence that the internal auditor found in the course of the examination (the current state).

- **Cause:** The reason for the difference between expected and actual conditions.

- **Effect:** The risk or exposure the organization and/or others encounter because the condition is not consistent with the criteria (the impact of the difference). In determining the degree of risk or exposure, internal auditors consider the effect their engagement observations and recommendations may have on the organization's operations and financial statements.

- Observations and recommendations can include engagement client accomplishments, related issues, and supportive information.

Criteria for Communicating (continued)

8. Conclusions and opinions are the internal auditor's evaluations of the effects of the observations and recommendations on the activities reviewed. They usually put the observations and recommendations in perspective based upon their overall implications. Clearly identify any engagement conclusions in the engagement report. Conclusions may encompass the entire scope of an engagement or specific aspects. They may cover, but are not limited to, whether operating or program objectives and goals conform to those of the organization, whether the organization's objectives and goals are being met, and whether the activity under review is functioning as intended. An opinion may include an overall assessment of controls or may be limited to specific controls or aspects of the engagement.

9. The internal auditor may communicate recommendations for improvements, acknowledgments of satisfactory performance, and corrective actions. Recommendations are based on the internal auditor's observations and conclusions. They call for action to correct existing conditions or improve operations and may suggest approaches to correcting or enhancing performance as a guide for management in achieving desired results. Recommendations can be general or specific. For example, under some circumstances, the internal auditor may recommend a general course of action and specific suggestions for implementation. In other circumstances, the internal auditor may suggest further investigation or study.

10. The internal auditor may communicate engagement client accomplishments, in terms of improvements since the last engagement or the establishment of a well-controlled operation. This information may be

Criteria for Communicating (continued)

necessary to fairly present the existing conditions and to provide perspective and balance to the engagement final communications.

11. The internal auditor may communicate the engagement client's views about the internal auditor's conclusions, opinions, or recommendations.

12. As part of the internal auditor's discussions with the engagement client, the internal auditor obtains agreement on the results of the engagement and on any necessary plan of action to improve operations. If the internal auditor and engagement client disagree about the engagement results, the engagement communications state both positions and the reasons for the disagreement. The engagement client's written comments may be included as an appendix to the engagement report, in the body of the report, or in a cover letter.

13. Certain information is not appropriate for disclosure to all report recipients because it is privileged, proprietary, or related to improper or illegal acts. Disclose such information in a separate report. Distribute the report to the board if the conditions being reported involve senior management.

14. Interim reports are written or oral and may be transmitted formally or informally. Use interim reports to communicate information that requires immediate attention, to communicate a change in engagement scope for the activity under review, or to keep management informed of engagement progress when engagements extend over a long period. The use of interim reports does not diminish or eliminate the need for a final report.

Criteria for Communicating (continued)

15. A signed report is issued after the engagement's completion. Summary reports highlighting engagement results are appropriate for levels of management above the engagement client and can be issued separately from or in conjunction with the final report. The term "signed" means the authorized internal auditor's name is manually or electronically signed in the report or on a cover letter. The CAE determines which internal auditor is authorized to sign the report. If engagement reports are distributed by electronic means, a signed version of the report is kept on file by the internal audit activity.

Quality of Communications

Communications must be accurate, objective, clear, concise, constructive, complete, and timely. Accurate communications are free from errors and distortions and are faithful to the underlying facts. Objective communications are fair, impartial, and unbiased and are the result of a fair-minded and balanced assessment of all relevant facts and circumstances. Clear communications are easily understood and logical, avoiding unnecessary technical language and providing all significant and relevant information. Concise communications are to the point and avoid unnecessary elaboration, superfluous detail, redundancy, and wordiness. Constructive communications are helpful to the engagement client and the organization and lead to improvements where needed. Complete communications lack nothing that is essential to the target audience and include all significant and relevant information and observations to support recommendations and conclusions. Timely communications are opportune and expedient, depending on the significance of the issue, allowing management to take appropriate corrective action (IIA Standard 2420).

1. Gather, evaluate, and summarize data and evidence with care and precision.

2. Derive and express observations, conclusions, and recommendations without prejudice, partisanship, personal interests, and the undue influence of others.

3. Improve clarity by avoiding unnecessary technical language and providing all significant and relevant information in context.

Quality of Communications (continued)

4. Develop communications with the objective of making each element meaningful but succinct.

5. Adopt a useful, positive, and well-meaning content and tone that focuses on the organization's objectives.

6. Ensure communication is consistent with the organization's style and culture.

7. Plan the timing of the presentation of engagement results to avoid undue delay.

Errors and Omissions

If a final communication contains a significant error or omission, the chief audit executive must communicate corrected information to all parties who received the original communication (IIA Standard 2421).

Use of "Conducted in Conformance with the International Standards for the Professional Practice of Internal Auditing"

Internal auditors may report that their engagements are "conducted in conformance with the *International Standards for the Professional Practice of Internal Auditing*," only if the results of the quality assurance and improvement program support the statement (IIA Standard 2430).

Engagement Disclosure of Nonconformance

When nonconformance with the Definition of Internal Auditing, the Code of Ethics or the *Standards* impacts a specific engagement, communication of the results must disclose the:

- Principle or rule of conduct of the Code of Ethics or *Standard(s)* with which full conformance was not achieved;

- Reason(s) for nonconformance; and

- Impact of nonconformance on the engagement and the communicated engagement results (IIA Standard 2431).

Disseminating Results

The CAE must communicate results to the appropriate parties. The CAE or designee reviews and approves the final engagement communication before issuance and decides to whom and how it will be disseminated (IIA Standard 2440).

The CAE is responsible for communicating the final results to parties who can ensure that the results are given due consideration.

If not otherwise mandated by legal, statutory, or regulatory requirements, prior to releasing results to parties outside the organization the CAE must:

- Assess the potential risk to the organization;

- Consult with senior management and/or legal counsel as appropriate; and

- Control dissemination by restricting the use of the results.

The CAE is responsible for communicating the final results of consulting engagements to clients.

During consulting engagements, governance, risk management, and control issues may be identified. Whenever these issues are significant to the organization, they must be communicated to senior management and the board.

Disseminating Results (continued)

1. Internal auditors discuss conclusions and recommendations with appropriate levels of management before the CAE issues the final engagement communications. This is usually accomplished during the course of the engagement and/or at post-engagement meetings (i.e., exit meetings).

2. Another technique is for the management of the audited activity to review draft engagement issues, observations, and recommendations. These discussions and reviews help avoid misunderstandings or misinterpretations of fact by providing the opportunity for the engagement client to clarify specific items and express views about the observations, conclusions, and recommendations.

3. The level of participants in the discussions and reviews vary by organization and nature of the report; they generally include those individuals who are knowledgeable of detailed operations and those who can authorize the implementation of corrective action.

4. The CAE distributes the final engagement communication to the management of the audited activity and to those members of the organization who can ensure engagement results are given due consideration and take corrective action or ensure that corrective action is taken. Where appropriate, the CAE may send a summary communication to higher-level members in the organization. Where required by the internal audit charter or organizational policy, the CAE also communicates to other interested or affected parties such as external auditors and the board.

Communicating Sensitive Information Within and Outside the Chain of Command

1. Internal auditors often come into possession of critically sensitive information that is substantial to the organization and poses significant potential consequences. This information may relate to exposures, threats, uncertainties, fraud, waste and mismanagement, illegal activities, abuse of power, misconduct that endangers public health or safety, or other wrongdoings. Furthermore, these matters may adversely impact the organization's reputation, image, competitiveness, success, viability, market values, investments and intangible assets, or earnings.

2. Once the internal auditor has deemed the new information substantial and credible, he or she would normally communicate the information — in a timely manner — to senior management and the board in accordance with Standard 2060 and Practice Advisory 2060-1. This communication would typically follow the normal chain of command for the internal auditor.

3. If the CAE, after those discussions, concludes that senior management is exposing the organization to an unacceptable risk and is not taking appropriate action, he or she needs to present the information and the differences of opinion to the board in accordance with Standard 2600.

4. The typical chain-of-command communication scenario may be accelerated for certain types of sensitive occurrences because of laws, regulations, or common practices. For example, in the case of evidence of

Communicating Sensitive Information Within and Outside the Chain of Command (continued)

fraudulent financial reporting by an organization with publicly traded securities, local regulations may prescribe that the board be immediately informed of the circumstances surrounding the possibility of misleading financial reports even though senior management and the CAE may agree on which actions need to be taken. Laws and regulations in some jurisdictions specify that the board should be informed of discoveries of criminal, securities, food, drugs, or pollution laws violations as well as other illegal acts such as bribery or improper payments to government officials or to suppliers or customers.

5. In some situations, an internal auditor may face the dilemma of considering whether to communicate the information to persons outside the normal chain of command or even outside the organization. This communication is commonly referred to as "whistleblowing." The act of disclosing adverse information to someone within the organization but outside the internal auditor's normal chain of command is considered internal whistleblowing, while disclosing adverse information to a government agency or other authority outside the organization is considered external whistleblowing.

6. Most whistleblowers disclose sensitive information internally, even if outside the normal chain of command, if they trust the organization's policies and mechanisms to investigate allegations of illegal or other improper activity and to take appropriate action. However, some persons possessing sensitive information may decide to take the information outside the organization if they fear retribution from their employer or fellow

Communicating Sensitive Information Within and Outside the Chain of Command (continued)

employees, have doubt that the issue will be properly investigated, believe that it will be concealed, or possess evidence about an illegal or improper activity that jeopardizes the health, safety, or well-being of people in the organization or community.

7. In a case where internal whistleblowing is elected as an option, an internal auditor must evaluate alternative ways of communicating the risk he or she sees to persons or groups outside the normal chain of command. Because of risks and ramifications associated with these approaches, the internal auditor needs to proceed with caution in evaluating the evidence and reasonableness of his or her conclusions, as well as examining the merits and disadvantages of each potential action. Taking this action may be appropriate if it will result in responsible action by persons in senior management or the board.

8. Many jurisdictions have laws or regulations requiring public servants with knowledge of illegal or unethical acts to inform an inspector general, other public official, or ombudsman. Some laws pertaining to whistleblowing actions protect citizens if they come forward to disclose specific types of improper activities. The activities listed in these laws and regulations include:

- Criminal offenses and other failures to comply with legal obligations.

- Acts that are considered miscarriages of justice.

Communicating Sensitive Information Within and Outside the Chain of Command (continued)

- Acts that endanger the health, safety, or well-being of individuals.

- Acts that damage the environment.

- Activities that conceal or cover up any of the above activities.

  Some jurisdictions offer no guidance or protection or offer protection only to public (i.e., government) employees.

  9. The internal auditor should be aware of the laws and regulations of the various jurisdictions in which the organization operates. Legal counsel familiar with the legal aspects of whistleblowing can assist internal auditors confronted with this issue. The internal auditor should always obtain legal advice if he or she is uncertain of the legal requirements or consequences of engaging in internal or external whistleblowing.

  10. Many professional associations hold their members accountable for disclosing illegal or unethical activities. A distinguishing mark of a profession is its acceptance of broad responsibilities to the public and its protection of the general welfare. In addition to examining the legal requirements, IIA members and all certified internal auditors must follow the requirements presented in the IIA's Code of Ethics.

Communicating Sensitive Information Within and Outside the Chain of Command (continued)

11. An internal auditor has a professional duty and an ethical responsibility to carefully evaluate all evidence and the reasonableness of his or her conclusions and decide whether further actions are needed to protect the organization's interests and stakeholders, the outside community, or the institutions of society. Also, the auditor will need to consider the duty of confidentiality imposed by the IIA's Code of Ethics to respect the value and ownership of information and avoid disclosing it without appropriate authority unless there is a legal or professional obligation to do so. During this evaluation process, the auditor may seek the advice of legal counsel and, if appropriate, other experts. Those discussions may be helpful in providing a different perspective on the circumstances as well as offering opinions about the potential impact and consequences of possible actions. The manner in which the internal auditor seeks to resolve this type of complex and sensitive situation may create reprisals and potential liability.

12. Ultimately, the internal auditor makes a professional decision about his or her obligations to the employer. The decision to communicate outside the normal chain of command needs to be based on a well-informed opinion that the wrongdoing is supported by substantial, credible evidence and that a legal or regulatory imperative, or a professional or ethical obligation, requires further action.

Communications Outside the Organization

1. The internal audit activity's charter, the board's charter, organizational policies, or the engagement agreement may contain guidance related to reporting information outside the organization. If such guidance does not exist, the CAE may facilitate adoption of appropriate policies that may include:

- Authorization required for reporting information outside the organization.

- Process for seeking approval to report information outside the organization.

- Guidelines for permissible and non-permissible information that may be reported.

- Outside persons authorized to receive information and the types of information they may receive.

- Related privacy regulations, regulatory requirements, and legal considerations for reporting information outside the organization.

- Nature of assurances, advice, recommendations, opinions, guidance, and other information that may be included in communicating information outside the organization.

Communications Outside the Organization (continued)

2. Requests can relate to information that already exists (e.g., a previously issued internal audit report) as well as for information to be created or determined, which results in a new internal audit engagement or report. If the request relates to information or a report that already exists, the internal auditor needs to determine whether it is suitable for dissemination outside the organization.

3. In certain situations, it may be possible to create a special-purpose report based on an existing report or information to make the report suitable for dissemination outside the organization.

4. Some matters to consider when reporting information outside the organization include:

- Usefulness of a written agreement with the intended recipient concerning the information to be reported and the internal auditor's responsibilities.

- Identification of information providers, sources, report signers, recipients, and related persons to the disseminated report or information.

- Identification of objectives, scope, and procedures to be performed in generating applicable information.

Communications Outside the Organization (continued)

- Nature of report or other communication including opinions, inclusion or exclusion of recommendations, disclaimers, limitations, and type of assurance or assertions to be provided.

- Copyright issues, intended use of the information, and limitations on further distribution or sharing of the information.

   5. If the internal auditor discovers information reportable to senior management or the board while conducting engagements that require dissemination of information outside the organization, the CAE needs to provide suitable communication to the board.

Overall Opinions

When an overall opinion is issued, it must take into account the expectations of senior management, the board, and other stakeholders and must be supported by sufficient, reliable, relevant, and useful information (IIA Standard 2450).

The communication will identify:

- The scope, including the time period to which the opinion pertains;

- Scope limitations;

- Consideration of all related projects including the reliance on other assurance providers;

- The risk or control framework or other criteria used as a basis for the overall opinion; and

- The overall opinion, judgment, or conclusion reached.

The reasons for an unfavorable overall opinion must be stated.

MONITOR ENGAGEMENT OUTCOMES

Audit monitoring and follow-up can be sophisticated or simple depending on a number of factors, including the size and complexity of the audit organization. Regardless of the type chosen, each audit should include: a firm basis for monitoring and follow-up actions, active status monitoring, and a determination of the results of actions taken on recommendations.

Auditee Responses

Auditee responses to the audit report are reviewed to assess their adequacy and timeliness and appropriateness of proposed corrective actions. Auditee responses and their corrective actions are monitored to ensure their timely completion. Effective follow-up is essential to get the full benefits of audit work. If monitoring and follow-up disclose that action on major recommendations is not progressing, additional steps should be promptly considered. Follow-up should be elevated to progressively higher levels of management of the organization to obtain prompt action. Continued attention is required until expected results are achieved. At this point, audit recommendations are closed.

Reasons for Closing Audit Recommendations

Reasons for closing audit recommendations include only one of these: the recommendation was effectively implemented, an alternative action was taken that achieved the intended results, circumstances have so changed that the recommendation is no longer valid, or the recommendation was not implemented despite the use of all feasible strategies. When a recommendation is closed for the last reason, a judgment is made on whether the objectives are significant enough to be pursued at a later date in another assignment.

IIA *STANDARDS* APPLICABLE TO MONITOR ENGAGEMENT OUTCOMES

Monitoring Progress

The CAE must establish and maintain a system to monitor the disposition of results communicated to management (IIA Standard 2500).

The CAE must establish a follow-up process to monitor and ensure that management actions have been effectively implemented or that senior management has accepted the risk of not taking action.

The internal audit activity must monitor the disposition of results of consulting engagements to the extent agreed upon with the client.

Effectively Monitoring the Progress

1. To effectively monitor the disposition of results, the CAE establishes procedures to include:

- The timeframe within which management's response to the engagement observations and recommendations is required.

- Evaluation of management's response.

- Verification of the response (if appropriate).

- Performance of a follow-up engagement (if appropriate).

- A communications process that escalates unsatisfactory responses/actions, including the assumption of risk, to the appropriate levels of senior management or the board.

2. If certain reported observations and recommendations are significant enough to require immediate action by management or the board, the internal audit activity monitors actions taken until the observation is corrected or the recommendation implemented.

Effectively Monitoring the Progress (continued)

3. The internal audit activity may effectively monitor progress by:

- Addressing engagement observations and recommendations to appropriate levels of management responsible for taking action.

- Receiving and evaluating management responses and proposed action plan to engagement observations and recommendations during the engagement or within a reasonable time period after the engagement results are communicated. Responses are more useful if they include sufficient information for the CAE to evaluate the adequacy and timeliness of proposed actions.

- Receiving periodic updates from management to evaluate the status of its efforts to correct observations and/or implement recommendations.

- Receiving and evaluating information from other organizational units assigned responsibility for follow-up or corrective actions.

- Reporting to senior management and/or the board on the status of responses to engagement observations and recommendations.

Follow-Up Process

1. Internal auditors determine whether management has taken action or implemented the recommendation. The internal auditor determines whether the desired results were achieved or if senior management or the board has assumed the risk of not taking action or implementing the recommendation.

2. Follow-up is a process by which internal auditors evaluate the adequacy, effectiveness, and timeliness of actions taken by management on reported observations and recommendations, including those made by external auditors and others. This process also includes determining whether senior management and/or the board have assumed the risk of not taking corrective action on reported observations.

3. The internal audit activity's charter should define the responsibility for follow-up. The CAE determines the nature, timing, and extent of follow-up, considering the following factors:

- Significance of the reported observation or recommendation.

- Degree of effort and cost needed to correct the reported condition.

- Impact that may result should the corrective action fail.

- Complexity of the corrective action.

- Time period involved.

Follow-Up Process (continued)

4. The CAE is responsible for scheduling follow-up activities as part of developing engagement work schedules. Scheduling of follow-up is based on the risk and exposure involved, as well as the degree of difficulty and the significance of timing in implementing corrective action.

5. Where the CAE judges that management's oral or written response indicates that action taken is sufficient when weighed against the relative importance of the observation or recommendation, internal auditors may follow up as part of the next engagement.

6. Internal auditors ascertain whether actions taken on observations and recommendations remedy the underlying conditions. Follow-up activities should be appropriately documented.

Resolution of Senior Management's Acceptance of Risks

When the CAE believes that senior management has accepted a level of residual risk that may be unacceptable to the organization, the CAE must discuss the matter with senior management. If the decision regarding residual risk is not resolved, the CAE must report the matter to the board for resolution (IIA Standard 2600).

TYPES OF FRAUD

Fraud is a generic term and embraces all the multifarious means that human ingenuity can devise, which are resorted to by one individual, to get an advantage over another by false representations. It includes all surprise, trick, cunning, and unfair ways by which another is cheated. Fraud is a term of law, applied to certain facts as a conclusion from them, but is not in itself a fact. It has been defined as any cunning deception or artifice used to cheat or deceive another.

The terms **cheat** and **defraud** include every kind of trick and deception, from false representation and intimidation to suppression and concealment of any fact and information by which a party is induced to part with property for less than its value or to give more than it is worth for the property of another. The terms **fraud** and **bad faith** are synonymous when applied to the conduct of public offenders.

Fraud can be classified in a number of ways from a discovery point of view. The reason for this classification is that different approaches and procedures are required to discover each type of fraud and to control each type's occurrence. Some types of fraud include: theft of assets, fraud by frequency, and fraud by conspiracy.

Controls to Prevent or Detect Fraud

Fraud prevention results in big savings because when fraud is prevented, there are no detection or investigation costs. This means a dollar spent in preventing fraud saves many more dollars later on. Therefore, greater attention should be paid to preventive controls.

Preventive Controls in General

Examples include: sharing the company vision with all employees; distributing fraud policies and programs; conducting proactive audits using discovery sampling techniques; database query facilities and data mining tools; and providing a hotline for fraud reporting by employees and others.

Detective Controls in General

Examples include: building audit trails in business transactions (whether automated or not); testing controls; conducting regular internal audits; conducting surprise internal audits; conducting employee performance evaluations; watching employee lifestyle changes; and observing employee behavior toward work.

Computer Fraud–Related Controls

Management (directive) controls, such as performing pre-employment screening procedures, requiring employees to sign a code of conduct, and conducting periodic training programs in computer security and privacy policies and procedures are good business practices. System-based preventive, detective, corrective, and recovery controls are also needed to efficiently combat computer crime and fraud.

Audit Steps to Detect Fraud

It has been said that most frauds are detected by accident, not by planned effort. This should not stop auditors from planning to detect fraud. Some known approaches to detect fraud include testing, statistical sampling, computer-assisted audit techniques, data query, and data mining tools. Some examples of tests include analytical techniques, charting techniques, recalculations, confirmations, observations, physical examinations, inquiries, and document reviews.

Steps to Take When Fraud Is Suspected

1. Document examination

2. Examining accounting records

3. Documenting fraud. Documenting fraud is a continuous effort from inception to completion of the fraud investigation.

4. Obtaining documentary evidence. Three principal methods exist for obtaining documentary evidence: subpoenas, search warrants, and voluntary consent.

5. Types of evidence. Evidence falls into one of two categories, either direct or circumstantial.

6. Organization of evidence

7. Charting techniques. Types of charting techniques for documenting fraud are link network diagrams, time flow diagrams, and matrices.

8. Business and individual records. Original documents are preferred and should be obtained wherever possible. If necessary, the examiner should furnish the record custodian a receipt for the property. If the originals cannot be obtained, the examiner can settle for copies.

Steps to Take When Fraud Is Suspected (continued)

9. Memorandum of interview. It is a good practice to write a memorandum addressed to the case file any time evidence comes into or leaves the hands of the fraud examiner or auditor. Whether it is included in the final report or working papers or not, each official contact during the course of a fraud examination should be recorded on a "memorandum of interview" on a timely basis.

10. Writing fraud reports. Reasons why a written report is so important include:

    - The report is an evidence of the work performed.

    - The report conveys to the litigator all the evidence needed to evaluate the legal status of the case.

    - The written report adds credibility to the examination and to the examiner.

    - The report forces the fraud examiner to consider his or her actions before and during the interview, so that the objectives of the investigation can be best accomplished.

    - The report omits immaterial information so that the facts of the case can be clearly and completely understood.

Steps to Take When Fraud Is Suspected (continued)

11. Characteristics of fraud reports. Important characteristics of good report writing include accuracy, clarity, impartiality, relevance, and timeliness.

12. Written report. There should be five major sections: cover page, witness statements, cover letter, working papers, and index.

13. Privileged reports. There is no privilege for investigative reports and notes, or for any fraud examination, forensic audit, or similar services. However, there are two exceptions.

    1. If the examiner is conducting an investigation at the request of an attorney in anticipation of litigation, the report is considered in most courts as an attorney/client work product that is, privileged.

    2. If a public authority, such as the police, federal agents, the courts or grand jury, or the like, is conducting the investigation, the report can be considered privileged.

14. Mistakes to avoid in writing fraud reports:

    - Conclusions. Under no circumstances should conclusions be made, as they may come back to haunt the examiner in litigation.

Steps to Take When Fraud Is Suspected (continued)

- Opinions. Under no circumstances should an opinion be written concerning the guilt or innocence of any person or party.

- Informant and source information. Under no circumstances should the name of a confidential source or informant be disclosed in the report, nor anywhere else in writing.

Legal Rules of Evidence

There are strict legal rules regarding the handling of evidence and the chain of custody thereof. If the examiner is operating under a lawful order of the courts that compels a custodian of records to furnish original documents, they should be copied, preferably in the presence of the custodian, before being removed from the premises. If not operating under a court directive and the records are being provided voluntarily by the custodian, the examiner may retain copies instead of originals.

The IIA *Standard* of Due Professional Care

The IIA *Standard of* Due Professional Care requires that a written report be issued at the conclusion of the investigation phase of a fraud case. It should include all findings, conclusions, recommendations, and corrective action taken or to be taken.

INTEGRATING ANALYTICAL RELATIONSHIPS TO DETECT FRAUD

Major Impetus

The major impetus for the need to integrate analytical relationships in detecting fraud was the recommendation of the Treadway Commission that analytical procedures should be used more extensively to identify areas with a high risk of fraudulent financial reporting.

The Treadway Commission defined fraudulent financial reporting as intentional or reckless conduct, whether by act or omission, that results in materially misleading financial statements. Fraudulent financial reporting can involve many factors and take many forms. It may entail gross and deliberate distortion of corporate records, such as inventory count tags, or falsified transactions, such as fictitious sales or orders. It may entail the misapplication of accounting principles. Company employees at any level may be involved, from top to middle management to lower-level personnel. If the conduct is intentional, or so reckless that it is the legal equivalent of intentional conduct, and results in fraudulent financial statements, it comes within the commission's operating definition of the term "fraudulent financial reporting."

Fraudulent financial reporting differs from other causes of materially misleading financial statements such as unintentional errors. The commission also distinguished fraudulent financial reporting from other corporate improprieties, such as employee embezzlements, violation of environmental or product safety regulations, and tax fraud, which do not necessarily cause the financial statements to be materially inaccurate.

Types of Analytical Procedures

- Trend analysis (i.e., identifying patterns and deviations)

- Ratio analysis (e.g., comparative ratios and single ratios)

- Modeling techniques (i.e., using simulation methods and sensitivity analysis)

INTERROGATION OR INVESTIGATIVE TECHNIQUES

Fraud Investigation

The objectives of fraud investigation are to determine whom, why, and how. Possible approaches include testimonial evidence, documentary evidence, physical evidence (forensic analysis), and personal observation; theft act investigative methods, such as surveillance and covert operations, invigilation (close supervision of suspects); concealment investigative methods, such as document examination, audits, computer searches, and physical asset counts; conversion investigative methods, such as public record searches and net worth analysis; and inquiry investigative methods, such as interviewing and interrogation.

Investigative Process

The investigative process consists of three phases, as follows:

Phase 1: Initiating the investigation—securing the crime scene, collecting evidence, developing incident hypothesis, and investigating alternative explanations.

Phase 2: Analyzing the incident—analysis of the evidence collected in the first phase along with alternative explanations to determine whether a crime has occurred.

Phase 3: Analyzing the evidence—preparing to present the incident with findings and recommendations to management or law enforcement authorities.

Team Composition

Investigating a fraud or computer-related crime requires a team approach with many participants. Each participant has a specific task to complete, consistent with their skills and experience. These participants (specialists) can include representatives from corporate investigations, law enforcement officials, system auditors, corporate counsel, consultants, IT security management, and functional user management.

Target

A victim organization should practice a "delay" technique when its computer system is attacked. If a system perpetrator can be delayed longer while attacking, investigative authorities can trace the perpetrator's origins and location.

Objects/Subjects

An investigation revolves around two things: objects (e.g., computers, networks, switches, processes, data, and programs), and subjects (e.g., former and current employees and outsiders, such as hackers, crackers, virus writers, cloners, and phrackers).

Software Forensics

The term **forensics** means using computer hardware and software to gather and analyze the evidence. Use of sophisticated **software forensics** may identify authorship of various code modules. By routinely analyzing modules on protected systems, substitution of valid software by intruders can be detected. This approach theoretically offers protection against attacks that would not be detected by network perimeter defenses, such as those that use covert channels, or attacks by internal users where those users are knowledgeable and sophisticated enough to circumvent normal host security. The possible benefit of this method must be balanced against the normally low probability of such an attack and the complexity of the defense, as well as its limits in detecting software modification, such as introducing Trojan horse programs.

Guidelines to a Successful Computer Forensics

- If one suspects that a computer system has been used in a crime, he should cut off its links to the network immediately.

- When evidence is found, it should be left untouched. This requires freezing or taking a snapshot of the computer records and data.

- Don't create a "reasonable doubt" situation to a judge or jury.

- Prove when each transaction has occurred with a time and date stamp.

- Protect the evidential matter (e.g., programs, data, and hardware) in such a way that it will not be modified, tainted, or fabricated. This is very important to the court.

- Store that evidential matter (e.g., data and programs) in an immutable form (e.g., tape or CD-ROM) so that it is inexpensive, defensible in a court, and easy to handle, present, and protect.

Use of Hash Algorithms in Computer Forensics

The idea is to collect as many different examples, versions, and updates of software as possible in order to generate file signatures for as many known files as possible. Each file within a package is "fingerprinted" by passing the file through a program that computes a hash code. The code is computed in such a way that if one bit in the file is changed, a completely different hash code is produced. The primary hash value used here is the secure hash algorithm (SHA-1). Several other standard hash values are also computed for each file. These include message digest 4 (MD4), message digest 5 (MD5), and a 32-bit cyclic redundancy checksum (CRC32).

When a computer hard disk, CD, or other storage medium becomes part of an investigation, the files stored on it can be "fingerprinted" using SHA-1, MD4, MD5, or CRC32. These fingerprints can be compared to the known file fingerprints in the NSRL's reference data set (RDS) database. Those files that have matching hash values can be discarded from the investigation without further examination; those that do not match the RDS database should be examined further. Expected files may be missing if they do not show up in the known file list. This may indicate that files were deleted to cover up illegal activity and may prompt the investigator to pursue other means of investigating the file system.

Search and Seizure

Ownership, occupancy, and possession are three influencing factors in a crime warrant search. A search warrant or court order is necessary to use the "trap and trace" technique, which involves the telephone company finding the intruder. Traps can be placed on in-circuit emulators, network protocol analyzers, and hardware analyzers.

If computer equipment involved in a computer crime is not covered by a search warrant, the investigator should leave it alone until a warrant can be obtained. A court order is also required to access the evidence and to conduct surveillance techniques. To get a court-ordered search, one has to show that there is probable cause to believe that the suspect is committing an offense and that normal procedures have failed or are unlikely to work or are dangerous to health and life. An independent judge must issue the court order, not a police officer, security investigator, law enforcement agent, or prosecutor.

Interrogation

During evidence collection activities, the investigative team interviews and interrogates many individuals. The interviewing and interrogation processes are quite different in terms of objectives, techniques, and timing. The goal of the interview is obtaining information about the incident. Here, the intent is finding the answers to the five Ws: *who, what, when, where*, and *why*. This requires talking to as many witnesses as possible. The goal of interrogation, however, is to establish enough evidence to consider the subject a suspect.

FORENSIC AUDITING

Auditing for fraud is called forensic auditing. The purpose of forensic examination (auditing) is to establish whether a fraud has occurred. One of the major purposes of financial auditing is to attest the financial statements of an organization. Unlike financial auditing, forensic auditing has no generally accepted auditing standards. In fact, most self-proclaimed forensic auditors are certified public accountants or internal auditors specializing in fraud detection.

USE OF COMPUTERS IN ANALYZING DATA FOR FRAUD AND CRIME

Collection and Preservation of Computer Evidence

Investigation of computer-related crimes more often than not involves highly technical matters, making it imperative during a search that appropriate steps are taken to ensure both the proper handling and preservation of evidence. There are seven recognized considerations involved in the care and handling of evidence.

1. Discovery and recognition

2. Protection

3. Recording

4. Collection

5. Identification

6. Preservation

7. Transportation

Chain of Computer Evidence

This section addresses various aspects of properly maintaining computer-related evidence. These procedures are important in avoiding problems of proof caused by improper care and handling of such evidence.

- Maintaining evidence in the form of computer storage media presents problems that differ from handling other types of evidence. Because they are subject to erasure and easily damaged, magnetic or electronic storage devices must be carefully guarded and kept under controlled temperature and humidity to avoid deterioration.

- In investigating and prosecuting a case involving such evidence, one of the early steps a prosecutor should take is to retain an appropriate computer expert or technical assistance. This can be critical in avoiding problems resulting from inept maintenance procedures or inadvertent loss of key information.

- Sometimes the contents of dozens or even hundreds of computer tapes or disks must be copied to allow the business to continue operating while the case is being prosecuted. This must be done under the close supervision of an expert who cannot only ensure that it is done right but can also determine the least costly procedure.

- Initials of the seizing agent and the date should be scratched on each storage media container, and a **chain-of-custody** sheet or log should be made for every container. The log should show, at a minimum, the date, place, and specific location of the seizure and the name of the agent making the seizure.

Computer Fraud and Crime Examples

- Military and intelligence attacks include espionage in the form of industrial espionage, economic espionage, and foreign government espionage.

- Technical attacks include wiretapping (electronic eavesdropping) and data leakage.

- Business attacks include employee sabotage, data diddling, superzapping of computer files, and spreading a computer virus.

- Financial attacks include salami technique, wire transfer fraud, and toll fraud through telephone cloning.

- Terrorist attacks include holding data as hostage and demanding ransom money for stolen data and programs.

- Grudge attacks include actions taken by disgruntled employees and the general public.

- Fun attacks include actions taken by people for challenge and publicity without money.

Appendix: Sarbanes-Oxley Act of 2002

The U.S. Sarbanes-Oxley Act of 2002 (SOX Act) contains provisions affecting the corporate governance, auditing, and financial reporting of public companies, including provisions intended to deter and punish corporate accounting fraud and corruption. The SOX Act generally applies to those public companies required to file reports with Securities and Exchange Commission (SEC) under the Securities Exchange Act of 1933 and the Securities Exchange Act of 1934 and registered accounting firms. This appendix contains only the SOX Act titles and sections that are of interest to internal auditors. Visit www.pcaobus.org or www.aicpa.org for SOX.

Title II of the Act addresses auditor independence. It prohibits the registered external auditor of a public company from providing certain non-audit services to that public company audit client. Title II also specifies communication that is required between auditors and the public company's audit committee (or board of directors) and requires periodic rotation of the audit partners managing a public company's audits.

Titles III and IV of the Act focus on corporate responsibility and enhanced financial disclosures. Title III addresses listed company audit committees, including responsibilities and independence, and corporate responsibilities for financial reports, including certifications by corporate officers in annual and quarterly reports, among other provisions. Title IV addresses disclosures in financial reporting and transactions involving management and principal stockholders, and other provisions such as internal control over financial reporting.

More specifically, Section 404 of the Act establishes requirements for companies to publicly report on management's responsibility for establishing and maintaining an adequate internal control structure, including controls over financial reporting and the results of management's assessment of the effectiveness of internal control over financial reporting. Section 404 also requires the firms that serve as external auditors for public companies to attest to the assessment made by the companies' management, and report on the results of their attestation and whether they agree with management's assessment of the company's internal control over financial reporting.

TITLE II—AUDITOR INDEPENDENCE

Section 201: Services Outside the Scope of Practice of Auditors

Registered accounting firms cannot provide certain non-audit services to a public company if the firm also serves as the auditor of the financial statements for the public company. Examples of prohibited non-audit services include bookkeeping, appraisal or valuation services, internal audit outsourcing services, and management functions.

TITLE III—CORPORATE RESPONSIBILITY

Section 301: Public Company Audit Committees

Listed company audit committees are responsible for the appointment, compensation, and oversight of the registered accounting firm, including the resolution of disagreement between the registered accounting firm and company management regarding financial reporting. Audit committee members must be independent.

Section 302: Corporate Responsibility for Financial Reports

For each annual and quarterly report filed with SEC, the CEO and CFO must certify that they have reviewed the report and, based on their knowledge, the report does not contain untrue statements or omissions of material facts resulting in a misleading report and that, based on their knowledge, the financial information in the report is fairly presented.

Section 304: Forfeiture of Certain Bonuses and Profits

The CEO and CFO of the issuer have to reimburse the issuer for any bonus or profits from sale of securities during the 12-month period following the filing of a financial document that required an issuer to prepare an accounting restatement due to misconduct.

Section 308: Fair Funds for Investors

The civil penalties can be added to the disgorgement fund for the benefit of the victims of a security law violation. A disgorgement sanction requires the return of illegal profits.

TITLE IV—ENHANCED FINANCIAL DISCLOSURES

Section 404: Management Assessment of Internal Controls

This section consists of two parts. First, in each annual report filed with SEC, company management must state its responsibility for establishing and maintaining an internal control structure and procedures for financial reporting; it must also assess the effectiveness of its internal control structure and procedures for financial reporting. Second, the registered accounting firm must attest to, and report on, management's assessment of the effectiveness of its internal control over financial reporting.

Section 406 (c): Code of Ethics

This section must provide for an enforcement mechanism and protection for persons reporting questionable behavior (i.e., whistleblowing). The board of directors must approve any waivers of the code for directors, executives, or officers of the organization.

Section 407: Disclosure of Audit Committee Financial Expert

Public companies must disclose in periodic reports to SEC whether the audit committee includes at least one member who is a financial expert and, if not, the reasons why.

About the Author

S. Rao Vallabhaneni is an educator, author, publisher, consultant, and practitioner in business with more than 30 years of management and teaching experience in auditing, accounting, manufacturing, and IT consulting in both the public and private sectors. He is the author of more than 60 trade books, study guides, review guides, monographs, audit guides, and articles in auditing and IT. He holds 24 professional certifications in business management in the Accounting, Auditing, Finance, IT, Manufacturing, Quality, and Human Resource fields.

Index

Index

Index